This book is the first study of the long tradition, ranging from Aristophanes, Martial, and Catullus to Rabelais, Pope, and Jonathan Swift, of using scatology as a satirical literary device in poetry and narrative prose. Although Swift resorted to it more than any other major author in English literature, his critics, when they have discussed it at all, have been mainly biographical or psychological. Dr. Lee, in contrast, examines scatology from a literary point of view, analyzing its rhetorical and thematic functions. He argues that scatology of itself does not make a work either "good" or "bad" as literature; it all depends on how effective it is as satire or humor.

Because Dr. Lee reevaluates writers like Martial, who are generally dismissed with clichés; because he shows that truly civilized people not only ought to but must be able to laugh at references to *skata;* and because his incidental comments reveal a deep sense of the necessity of sanity if human relationships are to transcend horror and disgust, his study has implications for all literature, especially that which is being today wrongfully attacked by the unknowing as obscene.

Swift and Scatological Satire

SWIFT AND SCATOLOGICAL SATIRE

BY

Jae Num Lee

Albuquerque

UNIVERSITY OF NEW MEXICO PRESS

 Manufactured in the United States of America by the University of New Mexico Printing Plant, Albuquerque. Library of Congress Catalog Card No. 76-129807.
SBN 8263-0196-7
First Edition

TO

PROFESSOR EDITH BUCHANAN

Acknowledgments

My first thanks are due to Professors Edith Buchanan, James Thorson, and Joseph Zavadil for helping me shape my argument and for offering valuable criticisms. My thanks are also due to Professors George Arms and Joseph Frank for their personal interest in my work.

I first began to think about scatology in general in my study of eighteenth-century literature under Professors Donald Greene and Hoyt Trowbridge. They pointed out the damages done to Swift's reputation by unsympathetic critics and the need to deal with scatology in its literary context. I am grateful to them for their encouragement.

In preparing this study for publication I owe the heaviest debt to Professor George Mayhew, who responded with characteristic incisiveness and generosity to every demand made on his time and on his vast knowledge of Swift. I am grateful to him for all the specific comments and suggestions he offered in our discussions and in pages of notes he prepared for me.

I wish to thank the entire staff of the Rare Book Room at the Henry E. Huntington Library for their ready and unfailing help in my research. The University of New Mexico and Portland State University have kindly provided me with grants-in-aid for my visits to Huntington. I would also like to thank Mrs. Lois Mock for her help in preparation of the Index.

To my wife, who has given me steady help and encouragement, I can only say thank you.

Jae Num Lee

Contents

Introduction

Swift makes use of scatology more than any other major author in English literature. Although many scholars agree that scatology is an important artistic element in his work, this subject has not been a topic of extended literary discussion. Despite the large body of criticism concerning Swift, a book-length study of scatology in both his prose and verse has yet to appear.[1]

Early critics were repelled by the scatology occurring in Swift's work. Among well-known critics, for example, Dr. Johnson pronounces a moral judgment against Swift, who "took delight in revolving ideas, from which almost every other mind shrinks with disgust."[2] Coleridge also refuses to consider Swift's uses of scatology as a literary device and disparages Swift's works "for the vast quantity of physical dirt with which they abound."[3] Taine declares that Swift "drags poetry not only through the mud, but into the filth; he rolls in it like a raging madman, he enthrones himself in it, and bespatters all passers-by. Compared with his, all foul words are decent and agreeable."[4]

If Dr. Johnson, Coleridge, and Taine strike us as unfair in refusing to consider scatology in the context of Swift's works, modern critics are hardly more judicious. When they discuss the topic, their approach has been mainly psychological. Aldous Huxley is one critic who isolates and uses the scatological elements in Swift's work for psychological criticism: "If the Yahoos were all his personal enemies, that was chiefly because they smelt of sweat and excrement, because they had genital organs and dugs, groins and hairy armpits; their moral shortcomings were of secondary importance."[5] Huxley concludes that the "hatred of bowels" was the "essence of his misanthropy" and that it "underlies the whole of his work."[6] J. Middleton Murry in his biography devotes a chapter to the scatological elements in Swift's work, but uses those elements primarily to elucidate and censure what he calls Swift's "excremental vision."[7] More recently Bonamy Dobrée asserts that "Swift could never become reconciled to human effluvia, to the notion that man is an organism that has to be voided." He goes on to theorize that "perhaps by deliberately facing the fact, he is absorbing some shock which has made his aversion to the physical almost if not quite pathological."[8]

Contrary to the opinions expressed by Huxley, Murry, and Dobrée, I believe that scatology in Swift's work merits study from a literary point of view that analyzes its rhetorical functions and the thematic purposes it serves. Because Swift consciously employs scatology as an effective literary device in his major satires and poems, it must be regarded as an important element in his work. As I have tried to suggest in citing representative critics, however, scatology has been a problem in Swift criticism. The problem is complicated because Swift does not regard scatology as a simple device of a fixed rhetorical function to bring about a single effect. Instead, he makes it a flexible device capable of serving various functions. While most authors would employ scatology exclusively for satiric purposes, Swift employs it for a certain kind of non-satirical humor as well.

Briefly defined, the problem of scatology in Swift's writings concerns what one can learn of his uses of scatological devices by a literary rather than a biographical or psychoanalytical approach. A biographical study by someone well trained in literature and psychoanalysis would be illuminating; a study of scatology as a literary device should be equally illuminating.

This study focuses upon the latter—scatology as a literary device. It is immediately evident that this approach assumes that scatology is neutral. Scatology as such does not make a work "bad" or "good" in a thematic, moral, or rhetorical sense. The author's skill and thematic purposes in handling scatology determine whether a work is "bad" or "good." Once we agree to adopt a neutral attitude toward scatology, we are able to examine its literary functions in a given work and divorce them from such extraneous considerations as the author's psychology or biography. This approach is based on an examination of literary precedents, where we find a genuine literary tradition of scatology in many European writings—English and continental—all of them known to Swift. An examination of this tradition indicates that scatology appears in more works than one may suspect; such an examination also reveals a clear literary tradition of scatological elements in European literature from Aristophanes to Swift.

This tradition encompasses two main uses of scatology, satirical and non-satirical. When we examine specific works, we discover that the satirical uses occur mostly in literary writings and that the non-satirical uses appear commonly in popular writings, such as humorous tales and jests. In a number of Swift's minor works dealing in scatological humor, however, non-satirical uses of scatology appear predominantly. These instances constitute the thorniest problems, because scatology is employed mainly for humor as an end in itself and not for serious thematic purposes. One such example is a verse-riddle "Because I am by Nature blind" (1724?). We can even approach this work on literary grounds because it has the tradition of scatology behind it. For, when we survey the early scatological writings—such as the medieval jests of *Howleglass* (1528?)—we can see that the verse-riddle fits into and continues the tradition of scatological humor.

Contrary to what one may readily expect, however, in the total body of Swift's work, this kind of scatological trifle is rare. On the basis of the canon of Swift's work, as edited by Herbert Davis and Harold Williams, I have found that "Because I am by Nature blind" (1724?) and another verse-riddle "The Gulph of all human Possessions" (1724) are the only pieces where scatology is used for the sheer fun of it. If we look closely at so blatantly a scatological work as *The Wonderful Wonder of Wonders* (1720), it turns out to be a guarded satire concerning the bank. Also, such poems as "The Problem" (1699) and "The Description of a Salamander" (1705) become satiric lampoons directed against historical persons. In Swift's major works some scatology is used for pure humor, but the satiricial uses of scatology far outweigh the non-satirical both in quantity and importance. This study, therefore, concentrates on the tradition of scatological satire as it appears in Swift's work.

The study is divided into two parts. The first part surveys notable scatological writings, verse and prose, of continental authors from Aristophanes to Rabelais, as well as English authors from Skelton to Pope. Aristophanes is the only dramatist represented, and he is included because the tradition of literary scatology begins with him. In this part of the study only those examples which best illustrate the tradition in which Swift was working are considered. The second part examines Swift's scatological writings, verse and prose, in somewhat greater detail. The more precise treatment given to Swift, however, is confined to the most pertinent examples of his uses of scatological satire.

The study is not intended to be an exhaustive catalog of scatological literature. On the other hand, if the cross-references in the footnotes seem overly detailed, my purpose is to suggest the extent to which scatological details appear in some of the writings my discussion surveys.

I have restricted the term "scatology" to uses of language referring, explicitly or implicitly, to *skata* and related matters, such as flatulency and privy. Consequently, I have excluded from my discussion such examples of quasi-scatology as halitosis, body odor, and filth unless they are employed in direct or indirect reference to *skata*.

In my use of the term "satire," however, I have been forced to adopt a descriptive definition sufficiently broad to include various kinds of satire. David Worcester in *The Art of Satire* appropriately labels satire as "the Proteus of literature" and points out that "the spectrum-analysis of satire runs from the red of invective at one end to the violet of the most delicate irony at the other" (p. 16). Because of this protean nature of satire, scholars are reluctant to provide a definition of satire in absolute terms. Instead, they describe its characteristic qualities. For instance, Frank Kernan in *The Cankered Muse* describes satire in terms of typical "scene, plot, and satirist."[9] One notable exception is Edward W. Rosenheim, Jr., who in his *Swift and the Satirist's Art* offers a concise general definition: "satire consists of an attack by means of a manifest fiction upon discernible historic particulars" (p. 31).

For my purpose, however, Rosenheim's definition in its entirety is too exclusive. The requirement of "a manifest fiction" would exclude polemics and diatribes; the requirement of "discernible historic particulars" would exclude satires on such general topics as greed and pride, particularly by writers of jests, characters, and epigrams. However, the requirement of "an attack" is a useful distinction that classifies writing lacking this element as non-satirical.

In reviewing studies on satire, I find this quality of "attack" to be one major characteristic common to various modes of satire, such as invective, burlesque, and ridicule.[10] For my definition of satire, therefore, I am borrowing an important portion of Rosenheim's definition: "satire consists of an attack." My definition would then become: "satire consists of an attack," "directed either to persuading us to look or act unfavorably toward the satiric victim or to pleasing us by the representation in a degrading manner of an object" (p. 31). By scatological satire I mean an attack delivered in words related to *skata*.

By humor I mean the amusing or laugh-provoking in the non-satirical sense. Scatological humor refers to the use of scatology for the purpose of producing laughter. It is in itself non-satirical. Humor, including scatological humor, is of course often employed for satiric purposes; for example, as a means of derisive ridicule. In such cases the context of my discussion should make clear the satirical character of the humor even though I do not use the word "satirical." For emphasis or clarity, when the character of humor is partially satirical and primarily non-satirical, I describe the humor by using the normally superfluous adjective "non-satirical."

In reference to works printed before 1750, unless otherwise noted, the place of publication is London.

1

Scatology in Continental Satirical Writings from Aristophanes to Rabelais

This chapter surveys the scatological elements found in some of the major continental satirical writings from Aristophanes to Rabelais. Though necessarily brief, the survey shows that scatology has long been an acceptable literary device and that, as such, it is "legitimate." The survey also points out the different ways that various authors use scatology to achieve their purposes. Six continental authors are considered. All six were well known to Swift as well as to many other English authors (discussed in the next chapter), who read these writers in translation, if not in the original, as part of the mainstream of their cultural tradition and inheritance.

Aristophanes was the first major author to employ scatology primarily for satiric purposes. Though he wrote comedies (the early Greeks did not have satire as a genre), he employed scatology as a device of censure and ridicule much as Roman authors did later. Of his eleven extant plays, *The Clouds* (423 B.C.) exhibits diverse examples of scatology as a device of ridicule. Aristophanes presents Socrates as the representative of the Sophists who teach "How one may speak and conquer, right or wrong."[1] The plot dramatizes the efforts of the hero, Strepsiades, to avoid—through sophistic argument—

the payment of his debts. Much farce and satire derive from the scatological images in the dialogue between Strepsiades and his teachers (Socrates and one of his students) in the course of their lessons on sophistic logic. A student of Socrates relates to Strepsiades the Master's theory concerning whether the gnats "Hummed through their mouth, or backwards, through the tail."

> *Student*. He [Socrates] answered thus: the entrail of the gnat
> Is small: and through this narrow pipe the wind
> Rushes with violence straight towards the tail;
> There, close against the pipe, the hollow rump
> Receives the wind, and whistles to the blast.
>
> *Strepsiades*. So then the rump is trumpet to the gnats!
> O happy, happy in your entrail-learning!
> Full surely need he fear nor debts nor duns,
> Who knows about the entrails of the gnats.
>
> *Student*. And yet last night a mighty thought we lost
> Through a green lizard.
>
> *Strepsiades*. Tell me, how was that?
>
> *Student*. Why, as Himself, with eyes and mouth wide open,
> Mused on the moon, her paths and revolutions,
> A lizard from the roof squirted full on him.
>
> *Strepsiades*. He, he, he, he. I like the lizard's spattering Socrates.
>
> (p. 279)

Here scatology is employed obviously as a device of ridicule, presenting the trivial and idle nature of the sophistic system of learning through the very nature of the problem Socrates deems important enough for discussion. At the same time the lizard's befouling of Socrates is comic in a highly satiric way. Though the Master may be a profound thinker, his gaze contemplating heaven itself, he is a ridiculous figure who does not know how to avoid a personal indignity. The episode points out the myopic nature of the Sophists by making fun of them and their learning. And the fun is hearty.

Aristophanes goes on to mock the atheistic thinking of the Sophists through further scatological images. Socrates compares the cause of rain and thunder to the flatulency that follows overeating. When Strepsiades claims that Zeus sends down rain and thunder, the Master denies his existence and scorns Strepsiades for being "so obtuse." Instead, the Master declares that the clouds precipitate rain and thunder "by Necessity strong."

> *Strepsiades*. Come, how can that be? I really
> don't see.
>
> *Socrates*. Yourself as my proof I will take.
> Have you never then eat the broth-puddings you get
> when the Panathenaea comes round,
> And felt with what might your bowels all night
> in turbulent tumult resound?
>
> *Strepsiades*. By Apollo, 'tis true, there's a mighty
> to-do, and my belly keeps rumbling about;
> And the puddings begin to clatter within
> and kick up a wonderful rout:
> Quite gently at first, papapax, papapax,
> but soon pappapappax away,
> Till at least, I'll be bound, I can thunder as loud,
> papapappappapappax, as They.
>
> *Socrates*. Shalt thou then a sound so loud and
> profound from thy belly diminutive send,
> And shall not the high and the infinite Sky
> go thundering on without end?
> For both, you will find, on an impulse of wind
> and similar causes depend.
>
> (pp. 301, 303)

As for the cause of thunderbolt, the Master explains that

> When a wind that is dry, being lifted on high,
> is suddenly pent into these [clouds],
> It swells up their skin, like a bladder, within,
> by Necessity's changeless decrees:
> Till, compressed very tight, it bursts them outright,
> and away with an impulse so strong,
> That at last by the force and the swing of its course,
> it takes fire as it whizzes along.

Strepsiades agrees, paying the Master a compliment by giving in similar language an anecdote from his personal experience:

> That's exactly the thing that I suffered
> one Spring, at the great feast of Zeus, I admit:
> I'd a paunch in the pot, but I wholly forgot
> about making the safety-valve slit.
> So it spluttered and swelled, while the saucepan I held,
> till at last with a vengeance it flew:
> Took me quite by surprise, dung-bespattered my eyes,
> and scalded my face black and blue!
>
> (p. 305)

Partly through scatology Aristophanes depicts the Master as an atheistic man with an obscene and deceitful mind, implying indirectly that all Sophists are similarly atheistic, obscene, and deceitful. Toward the end of the play, when Strepsiades' son, who also learns to argue with sophistic logic, insists that it is right to beat his father, Strepsiades recognizes the justice of the vexing situation and repents his own corruption. He admits that "It was not right unfairly to keep back/ The money that I borrowed" (p. 397). He denounces Socrates and his followers and sets fire to their "vile thinking-house" (p. 399).[2]

Of the Roman authors, Lucilius is usually given credit for writing the earliest satires. Horace maintains that Lucilius invented "a form untouched by the Greeks."[3] Horace further maintains that Lucilius studied Aristophanes with care and learned from the Greek master to what degree language may be realistic in satire and how bold a tone he might adopt.[4] Though Lucilius is said to have written thirty books of satires, less than 1,300 lines or scraps of lines remain today.[5] These fragments suggest the kind of unsparing and gross language Aristophanes used. One line reads: "So that if you wish to make a purging through the bowels, take care lest it should pour from your puffy body by all passages" ("ut si eluviem facere per ventrem velis, cura ne omnibus distento corpore expiret viis) (pp. 220, 221). Another line reads: "This fellow on the ground amidst muck and dirt and swine-dung of the sty" ("Hic in stercore humi stabulique fimo atque sucerdis") (pp. 350, 351). Still another line reads: "She stains you, but on the other hand he soils you" ("Haec inbubinat at contra te inbulbitat [ille]") (pp. 384, 385).[6]

In the degree of coarseness of language and boldness of tone, Catullus rivals his literary forebears, Aristophanes and Lucilius. Of his 116 extant poems, we may cite a half dozen with scatological elements (XXIII, XXXVI, XXXVII, XXXIX, XCVII, XCVIII) that both reflect the satiric tradition of Aristophanes and Lucilius and anticipate the later scatological satire of Martial and Juvenal. Unlike Aristophanes, who employs scatology mainly in attacking issues of public concern, Catullus employs scatology as a weapon of personal satire in attacking individuals of apparently little public importance. Though he uses more prurient language than scatology, when Catullus resorts to the latter, it becomes a formidable means of personal satire characterized by unsparing tone and revolting physical references. Poem XXXIX, for example, ends with a passage equal in coarseness to the later satirical epigrams of Martial:

> . . . nothing is worse
> than senseless laughter from a foolish face. But
> you're a Spaniard,
> and we already know the Spanish custom:
> how Spaniards clean their teeth
> and scour their gums with the same water that issues
> from their bladders.

> So if your teeth are clean, my friend, we know how
> you have used your urine.[7]

Indirectly the poem may be an attack on all men who, like Egnatius, always smile no matter what the occasion. Nonetheless, the immediate effect of the poem is personal.[8]

We can see the continuing tradition of satiric scatology in a handful of epigrams by Martial. As in the case of Catullus, the number of Martial's poems that we may classify as scatological in the strict sense of the term amounts to only a few. Out of some 1,500 epigrams, those with scatological elements number only about seventeen, and of these we may cite a half dozen epigrams as outstanding examples of scatology employed for purposes of forceful satire (I.37, 83; II.42; III.17; VI.81; XII.77).[9]

Like Catullus, Martial employs scatology mainly for purposes of personal satire, and like Catullus, Martial does not reject any word or image if it serves his purpose, no matter how revolting it may be. The stronger the satire, the more loathsome the figure of speech, and vice versa. In the following epigram (VI.81), for example, Martial employs the word "inguina" (middle) with its scatological connotation in suggesting the moral corruption of a person.

> You wash, Charidemus, as if you were in a rage with the people; such a cleaning you give your middle all over the bath. Even your head I should not wish you to wash here in such a fashion, Charidemus. Lo! you wash your head too: I prefer your washing your middle.[10]

More important than the literal meaning of the man's physical dirt is the implication of his dirt in the metaphorical sense. To the poet the dirtiest and most detestable part of this man is his head, the part that conceives evil schemes and despicable thoughts. The poet implies that Charidemus' moral and intellectual corruption is much more objectionable than his physical dirt. Though the key word "inguina" in its sexual and scatological senses is indecent, the purpose of the epigram is not lewd, but clearly satiric—a denunciation of an evil mind, made more powerful by the implicit scatological comparison.

If Martial attacks vices piecemeal, one at a time, through the short form of epigram, his younger contemporary Juvenal chooses an extended form of satire to tackle the whole of society in his assault on the various kinds of evil. Like most other satirists, Juvenal tends toward the exaggeration inherent in the genre. He depicts his society as the most wicked of all societies. He asks, "When has there ever been a heavier harvest of vice?/ When has the gut of greed swelled fuller . . .?" (I.87-88) He declares that "All vice is now at its height" (I. 149) and that "The future will find no worse morals to add, no new follies to try" (I.147).[11]

Juvenal's unbridled language reflects the invective tradition of Lucilius.[12] No subject or detail embarrasses or discourages Juvenal. Indeed he seems to have sought out the most indecent subject matter for targets of satire, which he couches in the grossest language. This unrestrained language heightens the emotional intensity of his protest. For he does not indulge in strong language for its own sake or for sensationalism, nor does he waste it on insignificant foibles. He directs his "verbal armory . . . upon faults deserving censure."[13]

The power of his satire lies precisely in its moral sense, which justifies scatology in its relentless attack on personal and social evils. While his ultimate aim is denunciation of vices, Juvenal employs scatology for various supporting purposes. He uses chamber pots ("metallae") as a debunking agent of satire. In his warning on the instability of human power he declares that power invites envy and drags some men to destruction. As a fearful example of this dictum, he singles out the downfall of Sejanus, the favorite of Tiberius. The crowd pulls down Sejanus' statue and melts it to make household utensils.

> And now the blazes leap
> And roar, with bellows in the forges;
> the head, by the crowd
> Adored, is burning, and mighty

Sejanus cracks; then out
of that face, once next to the chief of
all the world, are shaped
Pitchers, skillets, basins, and chamber
pots.
(X.61-64)

It is a triumph of tone that the final anticlimax of producing chamber pots out of the statue of the once-powerful man does not strike us as comic. The contrast between the chamber pot as a symbol of man's animal necessities and the statue as a symbol of human power is especially eloquent in its juxtaposition of the dangers and instability attendant upon power.

Like his predecessors, Juvenal also employs scatology for character defamation. His general method is to associate the object of his satire with a scatological detail, linking the two in an equation. The speaker in the Third Satire (*The Perils of Rome*) complains that he can no longer live in Rome because it is taken over by unscrupulous upstarts who will do any kind of work for money, even "unclogging sewers" and contracting for "flushing privies" ("conducunt foricas") (III.38). He also ridicules the Greek upstarts who will do anything to flatter their patrons. "Grin and a Greek laughs with you"; "Just say, 'I'm hot,' he'll sweat" (III.100-01, 103). A Greek will applaud a person "If he but belches deeply or, without wetting his clothes,/ He pisses straight . . ." ("si bene ructavit, si rectum minxit amicus . . .") (III.107).[14]

Similarly, in a variation of this method, Juvenal employs a scatological object (the chamber pot again) as a device of mockery. In denouncing the moral depravity of certain Amazonian ladies, he aims at a basic contrast between their delicately feminine appearance—"These are the girls who sweat in the thinnest of gauzy gowns,/ Whose delicate flesh burns even in silk" (VI.259-60)—and their rough masculine behavior:

But notice her sounds
Of grunts and roars as she thrusts a

sword, see how she bends
At a helmet's weight, how coarse and
thick the pads that defend
Her thighs!
(ll. 261-63)

He then makes a further contrast between these manly ladies and their femininity. Though they may act like soldiers with their swords, when necessity calls, they have to "squat on the pot" like all other women ("et ride positis scaphium cum sumitur armis") (l. 264). This is a telling scatological anticlimax, the main source of mockery.

Juvenal also resorts to scatology as a device of harshest condemnation. For instance, in exposing the ugly moral blemishes of certain Roman ladies, Juvenal employs the grossest language. He lets his audience witness some of the things the ladies do under the safe cover of darkness. Though they appear to be chaste, modest, and God-fearing, they are really unspeakably lewd, orgiastic, and blasphemous.

Come now, you wonder why Tullia
with puckered face sniffs the air,
What Maura says in her vile Moorish
foster sister's ear
When they pass the ancient shrine
of Chastity? It's here
They stop their litters at night and
piss on the goddess' form,
Squirting like siphons, and ride each
other like horses, warm
And excited, with only the moon as
witness. Then home they fly.
And you, setting out to greet fine
friends with dawn in the sky,
Will tread on the traces of your
wife's urine as you go by.
(VI.306-13)

Juvenal wastes no words here pointing out the specific vices these ladies commit. The image of the ladies' desecrating the goddess is by itself a shocking testimony to their blasphemy and a scathing attack on it.[15]

In Juvenal's verbal armory scatology is the strongest weapon of satire. A scatological passage or phrase or even a word expresses his censure to a marked degree. Because he never abuses or overuses it but employs it against vices that deserve the strongest censure, we cannot mistake the basic aim of his scatology, which remains moral and corrective throughout.

Though *The Divine Comedy* (1314-21) is not a formal satire, it belongs in this study because in the *Inferno* Dante employs scatology as a literary device to achieve a moral purpose. That is, by displaying the the nature of various sins he warns against them.[16] In Dante's scatological images, excrement serves as a major metaphor for sin. Other scatological words such as "fifth," "stench," "mud" ("lordura," "puzza," "brago") are variations of this basic metaphor.[17] This metaphoric conception may be explicitly seen in Vergil's reference to the various kinds of Fraud Simple as "all such filthy stuff." He explains to Dante that Fraud Simple includes

> Hypocrites, flatterers, dealers in sorcery,
> Panders and cheats, and all such filthy stuff,
> With theft, and simony and barratry.
> (XI.58-60)[18]

Dante's words for "and all such filthy stuff" are "e simile lordura." Besides "filth," "lordura" means "excrement" and "evil people."[19]

Throughout the *Inferno* the scatological imagery dominates the description of various sins, and Dante aims for recognizable similarity between the nature of the sin committed on earth and the nature of the punishment in hell. The sinner in hell relives his earthly life; the manner of suffering is simply a revelation of the nature of the sin. Thus the description of the punishment is also the description of the sin for which the guilty suffers. Simoniacs are planted with their heads downward in narrow holes of the burning rock with flames tormenting the soles of their feet that stick out in the air (XIX). We should remember that the rock here is no ordinary one. It is as Dante observes "the livid stone" (l.15) ("la pietra livida") of the malebowges (dirty ditches), the "ultimate province of evil,"[20] where other sinners grovel in filthy mire.

Not only the manner of suffering, but also the physical environment surrounding punishment suggests the nature of the particular sin.[21] Flatterers are steeped in filth (XVIII). The description of the setting emphasizes the loathsomeness of flattery.

> The banks were crusted with foul scum, thrown off
> By the fume, and caking there, till nose and eye
> Were vanquished with sight and reek of the noisome stuff.
>
> So deep the trench, that one could not espy
> Its bed save from the topmost cliff, which makes
> The keystone of the arch. We climbed; and I,
>
> Thence peering down, saw people in the lake's
> Foul bottom, plunged in dung, the which appeared
> Like human ordure running from a jakes.
>
> (ll.106-14)

The bottom of the lake where the flatterers are "plunged in the slop and filth which they excreted upon the world"[22] is so foul that it infects the entire surrounding area. The inference is easy to draw; if we do not want to be contaminated by such odious people, we should stay away from them.

Even anatomical details suggest the character of sin. The heads of sorcerers are twisted a full half-circle so that with the back of their heads above their chests they are forced to walk backward. This mode of punishment emphasizes "the twisted nature" of their magical art, "which looks to self instead of to God for the source and direction of its power."[23] Dante sees one of them with

> Our image so distorted, so bereft
> Of dignity, that their eyes' brimming pools
> Spilled down to bathe the buttocks at the cleft.
>
> (XX.22-24)

His mouth is located in the anal part. Sorcery is given the vile character of excrement and is associated with the devil, who is often depicted in medieval paintings as having a mouth in the anal part. We are not to listen to, and certainly not to seek, words uttered by such odious and devilish mouths.

Dante's purpose and logic in his use of scatology are unassailable. He employs scatology only in reference to sin—exposing, defining, attacking it. To him sin is the most hateful thing; consequently, the strongest possible attack must be made against it. Scatology is the logical choice because, by the very nature of its language, it simultaneously disgusts the reader, and condemns and attacks its target. It delivers the ultimate insult to anything or anyone. Hence Dante depicts sin as excremental and conceives of hell in scatological imagery. Dante's hell is one vast excremental dungeon. Nothing in it is clean or pure. The air is discolored, the water is syrupy filth, and the ground is miry, all fetid. At one point Vergil and Dante are so overpowered by the stench of hell that they are forced to pause to "grow used to this vile scent" (XI.4-12). It is a dark dungeon full of sighs and lamentations, utterly forsaken by God. There is no joy, no laughter, no hope. The sinners are punished through all five senses. They smell stench, they see demons, they taste mud, they hear cries, they touch the vile ground. It is a funnel-shaped dungeon with a downward progression of evil; the nearer the bottom, the graver the sin. At the bottom stands Satan, the arch traitor, frozen in the stagnant pool of Cocytus, farthest removed from God. The pool is the "Fundament of the world" (XXXII. 7).[24]

It is a measure of Dante's art that the *Inferno,* despite the preponderance of scatological imagery, never sinks to the level of sensationalism or farce.[25] The tone remains moral and didactic throughout. We are always aware of his serious purpose at every point in the work. Dante, the master of techniques, has turned scatology into a flexible, multi-functional device in the service of his serious aim. In his hands scatology becomes an instrument of denunciation, a device of definition, and a medium of didacticism.

The final author in this part of the survey is Rabelais. *The Histories of Gargantua and Pantagruel* (1532-64) is not a satire written in a consistent tone dealing with one clear-cut subject and one limited purpose. In a broad sense it projects a new attitude toward life, a new vision of the world. In projecting this new vision Rabelais employs scatology as a device for satirizing certain vices, certain institutions, and certain attitudes toward life.

At the simplest level Rabelais' scatology is funny and has little satiric significance. During the war against Picrochole, Gargantua's mare urinates, creating "a flood twenty-one miles wide," drowning a large band of the enemy.[26] One might point out that the incident ridicules through fantasy the absurdity of a man's waging war against another when he is so vulnerable and helpless in the face of sudden calamities such as this unexpected flood. The primary effect, however, is humorous;[27] and the first response is laughter, pure and hearty.

More typically scatology functions as a means of satire. The satire is not always readily apparent. At times Rabelais does not satirize his target directly or explicitly; rather, he approaches it in an inconspicuous way, in an incidental manner, often by way of digression. The scatological elements in such cases may strike us as non-satirical humor. On a closer examination, however, they are often found to be charged with satiric significance. The scatology in the sketch of the infant Gargantua at play seems at first sight to be merely stercoraceous.

> He was always rolling in the mud, dirtying his nose, scratching his face, and treading down his shoes; and often he gaped after flies, or ran joyfully after the butterflies of whom his father was the ruler. He pissed in his shoes, shat in his shirt, wiped his nose on his sleeve, snivelled into his soup, paddled about everywhere, drank out of his slipper, and usually rubbed his belly on a basket. He sharpened his teeth on a shoe, washed his hands in soup, combed his hair with a wine-bowl, sat between two stools with his arse on the ground, covered himself with a wet sack, drank while eating his soup, ate his biscuit without bread, bit as he laughed and laughed as he bit, often spat in the dish, blew a fat fart, pissed against the sun, ducked under water to avoid the rain, struck the

> iron while it was cold, had empty thoughts, put on airs, threw up his food or, as they said, flayed the fox, mumbled his prayers like a monkey, returned to his muttons, and turned the sows out to hay. He would beat the dog in front of the lion, put the cart before the oxen, scratched where he did not itch. . . .
>
> (I.xi.62)

If we examine the passage carefully, however, we see that it is a picture of a highly unconventional child at play. We see him doing all sorts of things he is not supposed to do. In fact his behavior is exactly the opposite of conventional. "He pissed in his shoes . . . sat between two stools with his arse on the ground . . . ducked under water to avoid the rain, struck the iron while it was cold . . . beat the dog in front of the lion, put the cart before the oxen. . . ." He is lord of himself, not at all bound by any rules except his own natural inclinations. From the point of view of the sixteenth-century man, this passage may be taken as a humorous satire on conventional behavior, folk-sayings, and proverbs.[28]

Rabelais' use of scatology stands out most forcefully, however, in more direct satire. In such satire scatology contributes directly to satiric intensity. Rabelais' satire of the conventional world view includes his ridicule of the medieval scholastic learning as represented by the Library of St. Victor. Pantagruel visits the famous library, which he finds "most magnificent, especially for certain books which he discovered in it" (II. vii. 186-87). He then gives us a long catalog of some of the books, some 139 titles. The satiric character of his catalog becomes immediately evident.

Most titles are obviously satiric:

> *The Codpiece of the Law*
> *Decree of the University of Paris on the Gorgiosity of pretty Women, for pleasure*
> *The Knavish Tricks of Ecclesiastical Judges*

It is a dozen scatological titles, however, that render Rabelais' ironic encomium of the library so dumbfounding in its mockery:

The Art of farting decently in public . . .
Tartaret, on methods of Shitting
The Greek prepositions discussed by the Turdicants
(II. vii. 187-90)

More typically in the attack on the philosophers belonging to the Queen of Quintessence and the monks, scatology seems to intensify direct and pointed satire. A good deal of the ridicule directed at the philosophers at the Home of Useless Knowledge (Mataeotechny) derives from satiric uses of scatology (V. xix-xxiii). The basic technique of ridicule is "reductio ad absurdum." Like Swift's scientific projectors the philosophers are engaged in incredible activities, such as extracting water from pumice and catching monster crawfish with nets in the wind. Unlike Swift's projectors, who try but do not succeed in their experiment, these philosophers carry out their schemes. But the uselessness of their achievement is pointedly ridiculed in the description of such an odious activity as "extracting farts from a dead donkey, and selling them at fivepence a yard."[29] Scatological elements like these make "reductio ad absurdum" so devastating.

Monks come under even more direct scatological attack and more explicit denunciation. Gargantua explains why "the frock and the cowl draw on themselves the opprobrium, insults, and curses of the world." "The conclusive reason," he asserts, "is that they eat the world's excrement, that is to say, sins; and as eaters of excrement they are cast into their privies—their convents and abbeys that is—which are cut off from all civil intercourse, as are the privies of a house" (I. xl. 125-26). On the strength of conventional metaphors associated with excrement, Rabelais here deals a double-edged blow. On one hand, he depicts the monks wallowing in the mire of sins; on the other hand, he implies that they are a devilish crew. If the monks "eat sins," they are devils and their abbeys a hell, the abode of devils.[30]

When we review Rabelais' uses of scatology, we see that he employs it very much as other authors do. Aristophanes employs it as a device of ridicule in humorous oblique satire, Catullus and Martial mainly as a device of personal satire, Juvenal as a means of strongest condemnation in attacking personal and social vices, and Dante as an instrument for denouncing and castigating various sins through full use of its conventional association with sin and its power to nauseate the reader. Rabelais exhibits more variety in the use of scatology than his predecessors; in fact, his uses include almost all the ends which scatology has previously served: humorous satire, ridicule, oblique satire, direct denunciation. Rabelais is unique, however, in employing scatology as an iconoclastic device. *Gargantua and Pantagruel* is, among other things, an expression of a new vision of human life, directed not upward to heaven but downward to man on the earth. This earth-directed vision of life is diametrically opposed to the conventional heaven-directed vision of life. Rabelais concentrates on general wrongs that constitute the foundation of the old world view. Through scatology he puts to flight the medieval; he heaps dung on useless philosophy; he beleaguers the oppressive walls of monasteries and the church.

It should be clear that scatology is a legitimate literary device employed in a continuing tradition by some of the most accomplished authors of all ages. Its flexibility is apparent when we see it used effectively in works as different in tone and purpose as *The Divine Comedy* and *Gargantua and Pantagruel*. The authors considered in this chapter have shown that scatology as such does not weaken, and certainly does not "degrade," the work. What determines the effectiveness and character of a work containing scatology is, as appears time and time again, the nature of the author's theme, the artistic purpose served by the device, and the skill with which the author employs it.

2

English Scatological Writings from Skelton to Pope

In the preceding chapter we saw various scatological literary devices that pre-Elizabethan writers used for thematic purposes. This chapter traces this tradition in English literature by citing outstanding examples of scatological writings before Swift. For convenience, we will examine scatology under two categories—satirical and non-satirical—by the various artistic and thematic purposes it serves. We shall see that these two categories are not equal in quantity or in the importance of their uses. Satirical uses—primarily for thematic purposes—constitute the main branch; the non-satirical—primarily for the purpose of producing laughter prompted by obscenity—occurs in popular writings. We shall also see that these branches of scatology in English literature develop in an asymmetrical pattern. This chapter, then, traces the development of these branches from Skelton to Pope.

Although the satirical writings outweigh the humorous writings in volume and importance, the non-satirical works merit equal attention. By first examining the non-satirical writings, we shall see the multiple purposes scatology serves and the extent to which scatology is employed. These non-satirical writings are important to an understanding of Swift's work because they will serve as a basis of comparison when similar works by Swift are discussed. They represent one kind of literary precedent for Swift's few non-satirical works that might be confusing to those who have no knowledge of this literary tradition in English literature.

NON-SATIRICAL USES OF SCATOLOGY

Though small in number, examples of non-satirical scatological humor appear in both literary and sub-literary popular writings often enough to form a thin but continuous thread of literary tradition.[1] These examples, however, appear as obscene jests much more frequently in popular writings than in literary. We may examine representative examples from popular writings under three groupings: the prankish, the flatulent, and the stercoraceous.

The jests in the first grouping—the prankish—concern retorts and hoaxes. The tone in these pieces is generally impish, and the scatological details are usually employed to ridicule the victim of the prank. In the jests involving retorts, we are invited to laugh at the cleverness of the hero and to enjoy the humiliation suffered by the victim. No. 101 of *Tales and Quick Answers* (1535?), "Of the same chaplain and one that spited him," is an early and typical example of this kind of jest. A shorter example is "On a living Warming-pan" in *The Complaisant Companion* (1674).

> A Citizen that was more tender of himself then wife, us[u]ally in cold weather made her goe to bed first, and when he thought her plump buttocks had sufficiently warmed his place, he then came and removed her out of it lay in it himself; and to make himself merry, called her his Warming-pan; she not being able to indure this indignity any longer, one night (Sir Reverence) she did shit a bed; he leaping into it, and finding himself in a stinking condition, cryed out O wife I am beshit, *no Husband,* says she, *it's but a Coal dropt out of your Warming-pan.*[2]

In the jests dealing with hoaxes, however, we are encouraged to laugh by way of ridicule, not so much at the malicious wit of the rogues who play pranks upon their victims, as at the stupidity of the victims, who are unable to counter dirt with dirt. No. 27 of *Howleglas*

(1528?), "How Howleglas sold turds for fat," is an example. The jest concerns Howleglas' selling "tallow" to a shoemaker. He fills barrels with turds capped at the top with a layer of tallow "as though it had been altogether grease." By the time the shoemaker discovers the swindle, the rogue, having sold his merchandise, is of course gone.[3]

The second group includes flatulent jests having to do with farting, which usually is the main source of humor in these pieces. Many of these jests involve crudely humorous or obscenely witty situations. Farting is a recurring detail in jests, particularly in earlier periods appearing in humorous writings of both popular and literary origins. Flatulent jests appear in most, if not all, collections of jests and facetiae with examples of scatological humor. They also appear in collections of epigrams, particularly the collections containing humorous epigrams. These jests usually generate stock response; we are to "grin and bear it," so to speak. Some are amusing, as the following title suggests: "How *Scogin* let a [fart], and sayd it was worth forty pounds."[4] Others are coarse in a witty manner, as in the following piece from William Hickes' *Coffee-House Jests* (1677):

> A Country Woman that was a bold Gossip, came to a Butchers in *Oxford*, and when she saw a Shoulder of Mutton hang up, she askt him what she should give him for it? He told her two Shillings and a half: *Two farts and a half*, says she: *Why*, says he, *give me two farts and a half and thou shalt have it: Say'st thou so Boy*, says she, *Why then have at it;* then she lifted up her pretty right leg, and let a good one, *Well*, says he, *there's one;* then sweet soul, she lifted up her left leg, and let another as good; then lifting up her two legs one after another, she let a lusty one; *Well*, says he, *there's three, but where's the half one? Why*, says she, *take which half you will of the last, for that was a rowsing one*. (pp. 155-56, no. 261)

It is interesting to note that farting seldom appears in "nasty jests" (the next group); it appears in more ordinary, less excremental jests.[5]

The last group we may call stercoraceous jests ("nasty jests"), which invite laughter by references to excrement, involving some pointless tale concerning elimination or crude wordplay. The distinction between jests in this group and those in the other groups lies in the degree to which scatology is emphasized. In stercoraceous jests, common devices, such as pranks and wordplay, are employed for the sake of excrement. The tone in these jests is generally nasty.

No. 101 of *Taylors Wit and Mirth* (1630), written, so the heading of the jests tells us, "on purpose to sticke in the teeth of my proud, squeamish, nice, criticall reader," is a piece involving a nasty countryman who insists on taking words at face value with deliberate disregard for common sense. He consults a physician about his sick wife. The jest concludes with the following dialogue:

> I pray thee, said the Doctor, tell mee in plaine termes how shee goes to stoole. Truly, said the fellow, in plaine termes shee goes to stoole very strangely, for in the morning it is so hard that your Worship can scarce bite it with your teeth, and at night it is so thin that you might eat it with a spoone.[6]

Jests in this stercoraceous vein do not have much point. Their main object is to elicit laughter by forcing excremental tales upon us so crudely that we are compelled to conclude that scatology is an end in itself, the main source of laughter.

We might briefly note here the use of scatology in fabliaux, another genre of popular writings. Scatology, however, does not dominate these tales; the total effect of fabliaux with scatological elements is more often comic or bawdy than scatological. For, in these relatively longer tales, scatological details do not stand out so dominantly as in short jests. Moreover, scatology is seldom employed as the primary object of attention. It is usually subordinated to other elements, such as the witty or the bawdy. This point holds true in both satirical and nonsatirical fabliaux, such as Garin's *Le Chevalier Qui Fist Parler les Cons* and *Bérengier au Lonc Cul,* and Chaucer's *The Miller's Tale* and *The Summoner's Tale.*

Examples of scatological humor of literary origin, mostly by authors under their own names, are mainly of two kinds—the flatulent and the stercoraceous. These pieces are, on the whole, versified jests, but belong to the tradition of scatological jests of sub-literary popular origin. Though not so numerous as those in popular writings, there are enough examples to form a discernible vein of scatological humor in literary writings. We shall first examine the flatulent pieces.

Farting seems to be regarded as an embarrassing accident in human behavior at which the bystander is supposed to laugh. It becomes an easy object of literary humor. Some authors comment on farting itself. Heywood points out its benefit in a couplet, "Of blowyng":

> What winde can there blow, that doth not
> some man please?
> A fart in the blowyng doth the blower ease.[7]

Others employ farting mainly to evoke laughter, especially in mixed company. The object in these pieces is good-natured, if embarrassed laughter. John Davies' epigram "In Leucam" is a typical example:

> Leuca in presence once a fart did lett,
> Some laught a little, she forsooke the place,
> And mad with shame, did eke her gloue forget,
> Which she returnde to fetch with bashfull grace:
> And when she would haue said, this is my gloue,
> My fart (quoth she) which did more laughter moue.[8]

Stercoraceous examples in literary writings emphasize excrement for the sake of laughter, as do examples of popular writings. The tone is nasty, as in jests, but it can be wittily nasty, as in the following epigram by Goddard which hinges on a mischievous pun:

> Page (quoth my Ladie) goe shitt the doore. The wind
> Whispers to lowde: a Tyrant tis I find
> And therefore shitt boye shit; shitt-too the doore
> Tis good lett badd guests out, but in noe more.
> T'vnhappie wagg (fraught with a knauish witt)
> Cryes, Maddam, tis not my office doores to shitt
> *Praie bidd your gentlewoman doo't: hir face*
> *Doth looke as yf shee would shit eurie place.*[9]

For a later example of this kind of pointless wordplay on excrement, we may glance at Herrick's couplet, "Upon Craw":

> *Craw* cracks in sirrop; and do's stinking say,
> Who can hold that (my friends) that will away?

The point of the couplet, if it has one, is that the craw is not talking about ordinary syrup; here it is "fluid faeces."[10]

Pointlessly excremental pieces of this kind, however, comprise only a negligible proportion of scatological writings, popular or literary. Except for *Howleglas* (with nine stercoraceous jests out of the total of forty-seven), of the collections of jests, facetiae, and epigrams I have examined, these excremental pieces number, in a given collection, at most only a few. On the other hand, we may note that though not numerous, they do not wholly disappear from humorous writings. Instead, they form a thin but stubborn vein that may be seen from time to time in scatological writings.

Even in a brief study such as this, we can discern a tradition of scatological humor in popular and literary writings. This is a minor tradition, to be sure, but it is a part of the tradition of scatological writings. Once we recognize this minor tradition, we can no longer dismiss scatological humor as an isolated literary phenomenon. Regardless of our personal taste concerning this kind of humor, we are obliged to treat it as a legitimate genre with a tradition of its own. If we do not recognize this tradition, we are likely to regard examples of scatological humor as peculiar to an author and proof of his diseased mind.

We note that this tradition is much stronger in popular writings than in literary. In sub-literary popular jests, uses of scatology for laughter are the rule; for satire they are the exception. In literary writings, the reverse is true, as we shall see in the remainder of this chapter. This contrast illustrates the point that scatology is a neutral literary device to be employed for different purposes. In popular writings, where entertainment of an audience is the object, scatology is employed mainly in humorous works of non-satirical character. In literary writings that generally have a serious purpose, non-satirical uses of scatology are exceptional, appearing mainly in humorous works.[11]

SATIRICAL USES OF SCATOLOGY

If non-satirical uses of scatology need apology, satirical uses do not. We have noted in the preceding chapter their prominent function in serious literary works in continental literature. We have seen that they serve important thematic purposes as a powerful device of ridicule, condemnation, and criticism.

In English literature, satirical uses of scatology are found in a greater number of literary works than one would suppose. They appear in both minor and major works of all the periods our discussion covers. By the time Swift inherits this tradition, it is well established in numerous literary precedents. In the rest of this chapter, I shall examine some of these precedents for a better understanding of Swift's uses of scatology.

Several approaches are possible: one is a chronological survey; another is examination by genre. I shall, however, adopt thematic categories. We have already noted the direct relationship between the thematic purpose and the rhetorical character of scatology, for thematic purpose determines the character of scatology and controls its uses. I shall examine satirical uses of scatology under four categories: (1) personal satire, (2) socio-political satire, (3) religio-moral satire, and (4) intellectual satire.

Personal Satire

In a broad sense, most satires directed against individuals are personal. The distinction between personal satire here and other satires directed against persons lies in the degree of personal relevance to the individual satirized. If an author attacks an individual primarily as a projector, for example, I consider the work under social satire. If he attacks an individual for personal reasons, I classify the work under personal satire.

Because of the nature of language, scatology is a particularly devastating device of personal satire. It functions often as a means of lowering personal reputation to the level of dirt or even equating a person to the most loathsome object shunned by all. One of the strongest devices of censure, it is not to be employed lightly. Nonetheless, a number of scathing personal satires written in scatological language belong to the periods we are considering.

Among longer poems, we have Skelton's *Poems Against Garnesche* (1513-14).[12] Skelton identifies the target of his satire and delivers his attack directly in reference to specific wrongs committed against him. Skelton charges that Garnesche, a gentleman-usher to Henry VIII (p. 153n.), had insulted him in the court, calling him a "lorell," disparaging his ancestry, scorning his laureateship. Skelton's attack is a virulent invective rendered in part in scatological details. Skelton does not rely heavily on scatology, but intersperses his denunciation with scatological details.

The satire is mercilessly personal. He scorns the lowly origin of Garnesche, who as a boy was a "kitchin-page,/ A dish-washer" (p. 154). He draws an ugly portrait of his enemy, including his "wind-shaken shanks . . . long loathly legs,/ Crooked as a camock, and as a cow calfless," his "tawny" teeth, glassy eyes, "loathsome lere . . . like a greased boot" (p. 151). He hurls the charge of ill smell:

> Your breath it is so fell
> And so puauntly doth smell,
> And so heinously doth stink,
> That neither pump nor sink
> Doth savour half so sour
> Against a stormy shower.
>
> (p. 157)

Still not content, Skelton flings out a catalog of animals in name-calling, characteristic of *ad hominem* satire: "Thou toad, thou scorpion,/ Thou bawdy babion . . ." (p. 158). He goes on to name a dozen beasts, reinforcing the prevalent animal imagery of the poem, calculated to debase his enemy to the level of foul beasts. Deriding Garnesche by saying that "Thy mirror may be the devil's arse" (p. 160), he adds scornfully that

> It 'comes thee better for to drive
> A dung-cart or a tumbrel
> Than with my poems for to mell.
>
> (p. 162)

He is certain that the famous satirists of the past "As Persius and Juvenal,/ Horace and noble Martial," would all write of his enemy "The foulest sloven under heaven" (p. 163). Though the poem would be a strong invective without scatology, it is stronger because of scatology. Though scatology is not the major device of invective, Skelton uses it forcefully for ridicule and diatribe that help to establish and maintain an attitude of utter contempt toward the subject. The poem is marked by a fearless tone, but Skelton is too good an artist to indulge in scatology for its own sake. His artistic control unobtrusively enriches the texture of the animal imagery.[13]

Among short poems, we have an outstanding epigram in Jonson's "A Little Shrub Growing By," which is superior to any other poem of its class in English and is equal to the best Latin epigrams. Because an epigram is usually short and formal, its satire is of necessity direct. While losing the cumulative effect of more prolonged attack possible in a lengthier satire, the shorter epigram carries the concentrated force of a well-placed sting, direct and to the point.

> Aske not to know this Man. If fame should speake
> His name in any mettall, it would breake.
> Two letters were enough the plague to teare
> Out of his Grave, and poyson every eare.
> A parcell of Court-dirt, a heape, and masse
> Of all vice hurld together, there he was,
> Proud, false, and trecherous, vindictive, all
> That thought can adde, unthankfull, the lay-stall
> Of putrid flesh alive! of blood, the sinke!
> And so I leave to stirre him, lest he stinke.[14]

The image is concrete in detail, the style plain and sententious, the language masculine with its low scatological words and sinewy verbs, and the sound of the verse appropriately rough. If a similar effect could be managed in half the length, this would rank among the finest satirical epigrams in any language.[15]

Of prose works in this category, the quarrel between Gabriel Harvey and Thomas Nashe provides us with outstanding examples. Though the works by both parties in this quarrel contain scatological elements to varying degrees, we shall examine the most scatological of these works in Nashe's *Haue with You to Saffron-Walden* (1596).[16]

Nashe employs scatology, as does Harvey, as the ultimate weapon of insult. Though *Saffron-Walden* is a lengthy work, he resorts to scatology frequently in his vituperation and belittling of the Harvey brothers. Not surprisingly, the tone is extremely bold and the mood combatively abusive. He confronts the Harveys directly and treats them mainly in excremental imagery. The account of Gabriel Harvey's birth is fairly typical of Nashe's bold use of scatology in personal satire:

> Whether it be verifiable, or onely probably surmised, I am vncertaine, but constantly vp and downe it is bruted, how he pist incke as soone as euer hee was borne, and that the first cloute he fowld was a sheete of paper; whence some mad wits giu'n to descant, euen as *Herodotus* held that the *Aethiopians* seed of generation was as blacke as inke, so haply they vnhappely wold conclude, an *Incubus,* in the likenes of an inke-bottle, had carnall copulation with his mother when hee was begotten.[17]

In "these bitter-sauced Inuectiues" (p. 18), Nashe also befouls those who side with Harvey. He asserts that the Harvey brothers are "the most contemptible *Mounsier Aiaxes* of excrementall conceipts and stinking kennel-rakt vp inuention that this or anie Age euer afforded" (p. 11). As for the company Harvey keeps, "hee hath made as ill choyce of frends as of enemies; seeking, like the Panther, to cure himselfe with mans dung, and with the verie excrements of the rubbishest wits that are, to restore himselfe to his bloud, and repaire his credit and estimation" (p. 108). With such friends "hee cannot chuse but bee sixtie times a more poore Slauonian arse-worme" (p. 109).[18]

His scatological vituperation is total, including his treatment of Harvey's intellectual activities. In reference to Harvey's scholarly career, Nashe calls him "speciall superuisor of all excrementall superfluities for Trinitie Colledge in Cambridge" (p. 5). As for the literary career of the Harvey brothers, "witlesse Gabriel and ruffling Richard," Nashe sarcastically comments that "for anie time this foure and twentie yeare they haue plaid the fantasticall gub-shites and goose-giblets in

Print."[19] On the same page, their writing is referred to as "their filthie dull-headed practice" (p. 12). The act of Harvey's writing is seen as an act of defecation; "dungd vp" (p. 35) and "muckehill vp" (p. 122) are two figurative verbs Nashe employs in referring to Gabriel's attacks upon him.[20]

The strongest use of scatology is made against the person of Harvey. Because it involves the juxtaposition of excrement and palate, it is particularly revolting and forceful. Nashe does not often indulge in this extreme form of personal satire, but the few references he makes are conspicuous. At first, Nashe employs this extreme scatology against Harvey's patrons, hinting broadly that the sort of person who would patronize Harvey may be a man of feeble intellect and loose moral character who might "doo anie thing," even "sucke figges out of an asses fundament" (p. 42). Later, in denying Harvey's vexing charge of plagiarism, Nashe again uses this extreme form of personal satire. He declares that "like a iakes barreller . . . he girds me *with imitating of* Greene, let him vnderstand, I more scorne it than to haue so foule a iakes for my groaning stoole as hys mouth" (p. 132). As a final insult, he taunts Harvey with a threat of "cramming a turd in his iawes" next time they should confront each other and assures him that he has "bespoken a boy and a napkin already to carry it in" (p. 134).[21]

The remarkable point about the scatological elements in *Saffron-Walden* is Nashe's refusal to employ scatology for its own sake. No matter how loathsome his writing may become at times, his purpose is always clearly satirical. The same holds true for Harvey. In their quarrel, both employ scatology as an ultimate weapon of satire; they do not abuse it or waste it for frivolous entertainment.[22] Though one may dislike the scatological elements in their writings for personal or aesthetic reasons, he cannot fail to recognize that they use scatology primarily as a legitimate literary tool.

Socio-Political Satire

In the second group of scatological examples, those of socio-political satire, three targets are prostitutes, projectors, and the anti-Royalist Party. Because it is a highly revolting device of personal attack, scatology is frequently employed by various authors against prostitutes. It is particularly effective as a device to evoke emotions of disgust and shock. This power of scatology to shock and disgust may best be seen when it is compared with non-scatological examples. Thomas Fuller's character of "The Harlot" in *The Profane State* (1642) opens with the sentence, "The harlot is one that her self is both merchant and merchandise, which she selleth for profit, and hath pleasure given her into the bargain, and yet remains a great loser."[23] The opening line of Francis Lenton's character of "An Old Bawd" is much more forceful for being scatological: "An old bawd is a menstrous beast, engendred of divers most filthy excrements, by the stench of whose breath the Ayre is so infected, that her presence is an inevitable contagion. . . ."[24] To make another comparison, one of the metaphors "J. H." employs in his character of "A Whore" is "a Barbers chaire, as soon as one is out, another is in."[25] Lenton's scatological metaphor, however, is at once revolting: a prostitute "may be compar'd to a Jakes, which every rogue useth for necessity, and then abhorres it."[26]

This reference to a jakes is interesting, if disgusting, because it implies that prostitutes are necessary evils. John Taylor in *A Bawd* (1635) dwells on this point, satirizing both the bawd and her patrons, since only corrupt men submit themselves to this "necessity."

> We doe esteeme a *Fountaine, Well,* or *Spring* to be the most cleere from poyson, if a Toad, a Newt, or a snake, be in either of them, for we imagine that those venimous creatures doe sucke or extract all the contagion of that Christaline Element into themselves. In the like nature, a *Bawd* is the snuffers of the Common-wealth, and the most wholesome or necessary Wheele-barrow or Tumbrell, for the close conveyance of mans luxurious nastinesse, and sordid beastiality. Ravens, Kites, Crowes, and many other birds of prey, are tolerated to live unhurt, not for any good that is in themselves, but because they doe good offices in devouring and carrying away our Garbage and noysome excrements, which they live by: and if they were not our voluntary Scavengers, we should be much annoyed with contagious savours of these corrupted

> offals. These are the right paternes of an industrious *Bawd*, for shee pickes her living out of the laystall or dunghill of our vices; if she thrive and grow fat, it is with the *Merdurinous* draffe of our imperfections, (for shee is seldome beholding to an honest man for so much as a meales meat) she robs not the vertuous of any part of their virtue, she lives only by the vicious, and in this sort she is an executioner of sinners, and in the end gives the most wicked cause to repent, leaving them such aking remembrance in their joynts, that their very bones rattle in their skins.[27]

Though employed commonly, scatological metaphors for prostitutes remain powerful, because we do not, as a rule, associate the female with anything so odious or revolting. They also suggest decay, filth, and contagion. In these satires, one is often made to feel that he contaminates himself and becomes malodorous in physical contact with these "venimous creatures."

In satire against projectors,[28] scatology is employed primarily as a device of ridicule rather than shock. One reason is that scatology is used conventionally for sarcasm and invective against almost any profession. Another reason is based on the kind of excremental schemes some of the projectors advertised, which, to most men of common sense, appeared highly dubious or wild. Hugh Platt, for instance, in *Diuerse New Sorts of Soyle not yet Brought into any Publique Vse, for Manuring both of Pasture and Arable Ground* (1594) advises his audience that he "heard some studious practisers very confidently affirm" how one could harvest a rich crop of corn by using the seeds steeped in water "wherein good store of Cow dung hath lyen in imbibition, for certaine daies (which times you must also serch, if you meane to be an exact maister) . . ." (pp. 35-36). In *A New, Cheape and Delicate Fire of Cole-Balles* (1603), Platt also suggests the possibility of making fuel out of "seacole and Cowdunge," which he found "maketh a sweete and pleasing fire."[29] Some forty years later an anonymous projector in *Artificiall Fire, or, Coale for Rich and Poore* (1644) takes up the same subject and proposes "the manufacture of charcoal from coal and clay or dung or peat. . . ."[30] Gabriel Plattes, in *The Profitable Intelligencer* (1644), claims that "letting dung accumulate in double houses of office would also permit the manufacture of saltpetre for fertilizer."[31]

We need not inquire whether these schemes have in fact real merit. The point is that to their contemporaries the projectors of these schemes appeared ludicrous or fantastic. The scoffing satirists returned compliments by parodying their schemes, by flinging back the dirt, so to speak. Thus Thomas Heywood in a satiric character of the projector in his *Machiavels Ghost. As He lately Appeared to his Deare Sons, the Moderne Projectors* (1641) gleefully asserts that a projector is "one whose Arse makes buttons by the Bushell at the noyse of a Parliament, more than the *Scots* do at the noyse of *English* Drummes . . ." (sig. C3), that "The Ragge-Projectors, were extracted from Dung-hills, the out-casts of a Brokers Fripperie. In Long Lane they tooke their originals, and 'tis believed their endings will be in Houndsditch" (sig. D2).[32]

Some schemes are so preposterous that the satirist need not parody them. Thomas Brugis in *The Discovery of a Proiector* (1641) chooses to assail his victim through recitation which, in this instance, turns out to be a far more effective means of satire than violent diatribe or parody. He recites various projects he has heard, such as the invention of a "Woodden Horse, that with Scrues and Devises should travell further in a day by much then the *Dromedaries* . . ." (p. 24). In the course of repeating these marvellous inventions, he cites the case of another projector, "a very notable one,"

> who pretended to lengthen life also by removing ill savours; And to this end his ingenuous *Projecting* braine devised that every man, and woman within the City of *London* should imploy two boxes made very close of Wood to keepe in the smell, and these must be removed with Carts every two dayes, and then brought againe being discharged, and cleansed; and for these his extraordinary paines, and charges, hee would have but a penny a Weeke of every house, onely the chiefest gaine he expected was out of that which he carried away, whereof hee intended to make

> Saltpeter, and so furnish the Realme extraordinarily with Gunpowder; this was not very well liked by the Goldfinders, for had it gone on, they must of necessity have turned Saltpetermen, because they know no other trade but what concerned such stinking businesse. (pp. 25-26)

To make this satire even more scathing, all one needs to do is to distort and exaggerate this extraordinary scheme as Rabelais or Swift would have done.[33]

In political satire, the major target of scatological assault is the anti-Royalist Party, the Parliamentarian party popularly known as the Rump parliament. Because of its derisive connotations, the word "rump" lends itself easily to mockery. While its primary meaning denotes an anatomical part of the body, its secondary meaning suggests the remnant of a whole, often in the sense of an undesirable leftover of little worth. The term as employed in reference to the Parliamentarian party also carries the implication of an undesirable, unimportant, contemptible political minority, not representative of the nation, and therefore unauthoritative. Some of these negative connotations and associations are most contemptuously used in the opening sentence of *The Character of the Rump* (1660) remarkable for its devastating scatological thrust. The anonymous author declares that

> A Rump is the hinder part of the many-headed Beast, the Back-door of the *Devils Arse* a *Peake,* Tyranny and Rebellion ending in a Stink, the States *Incubus,* a Crab Commonwealth with the But-end formost; 'tis a Town-ditch swelling above the walls, a Sink taking possession of the whole House, the Humours left behind after the substance of the Body politick is purg'd away by the devils potions, the Tumour of the Breech, *Caninus Apetitus in Ano,* the Epilogue grown greater then the Play, the Close of the Will crept into the place of *In nomine Dei Amen,* the Whore of *Babylon* with her Arse upwards, 'tis like a Comet which is all tail, and portends no lesse mischief, or you may call it the tail of the Great Dragon, and 'tis a Thumper, for the devils tail in

Chaucer, being stuck in this, would look but like a maggot in a Tub of Tallow, and yet he saith

That certainly Sathanas hath such a Tail
Broader then of a Pinnace is the Sail.[34]

Similarly, in their attacks on the Parliamentarian party, the satirists of the Royalist party or those sympathetic to the Royalist cause assumed a common mood of contempt and mockery. For instance, the anonymous author in *Bibliotheca Fanatica* (1660) ridicules the Rump by citing mock titles of books. This work is reminiscent of Rabelais' satire of medieval scholastic learning as represented by the Library of St. Victor. The tone in *Bibliotheca Fanatica* is not ironic, as in Rabelais' mocking encomium of the "most magnificent" library, but its method of cataloging real and fictitious books for the purposes of satire is the same. Though the catalog is not so nearly scatological as Rabelais', it does include a few titles that deftly deliver stinging jibes at the anti-Royalist Party: "Babylon is fallen, Babylon is fallen: or, the true Relation of the final Overthrow, and utter Destruction of the rotten Rump of a Parliamentary Junto, by a Friend to King Charles the Second"; "Lucri bonus est odor ex re qualibet; a Treatise written in Defence of his seizing on the Boy's Close-stool Pan, and reserving the Contents for his own Profit, because the Lad was so profane to carry it on a Sunday; by Alderman Atkins, Shit-breeches"; "Fistula in Ano, and the Ulcer of the Rump; wherein is shewn, that there is no better Way to cure such Distempers, than a Burning, or Cauterising; by the Rump-confounding Boys of the City of London" (pp. 142-43).[35]

In stronger scatological attacks, many authors pointedly capitalize on the anatomical associations of the word by stressing the base, contemptible, and odious nature of the Parliamentarians. Thus, we see the derision of the word in the following jest, which concludes with a scatological figure of the Rump:

A Company of confident Blades were each of 'em bragging what they durst do, and how they wou'd go upon any exploit. *Puh,* says one among 'em, *ye are all Punges to me; for I dare go where a Prince cannot send his Embassadour*. They then askt him where that was? He said, *To go to stool; for though an Embassadour represents the Kings person, yet he cannot do his business for him that way. Yes, yes,* say they, *we smell your conceit, and therefore think you a Fanatick; for it savours too much of the Rump.*[36]

The scatological associations of the Rump are heavily exploited in satirical verses on the anti-Royalist Party by anonymous authors. Though some verses direct their sting to specific individuals, they are not for that reason alone to be classified under personal satire. Since the emphasis of the attack is contempt for these individuals as members of the Parliamentarian party such verses are obviously political satire. The following satire "Upon the Parliament Fart" in Alexander Brome's anthology, *Rump: or an Exact Collection of the Choycest Poems and Songs Relating to the Late Times* (1662), is an example of a more pointed scatological mockery of the Parliamentarians. The first sixteen lines are typical of the satiric quality of the entire poem.

Down came Grave Antient Sir *John Crooke,*
And read his Messuage in a Book;
Very well quoth *Will. Norris,* it is so,
But Mr. *Pym*'s Tayle cry'd No.
Fye quoth Alderman *Atkins* I like not this passage,
To have a Fart inter voluntary in the midst of a Message.
Then upstarts one fuller of Devotion
Than Eloquence, and said, a very ill Motion,
Not so neither quoth Sir *Henry Jenking,*
The Motion was good but for the stinking.
Quoth Sir *Henry Poole* 't was an audacious trick
To fart in the face of the Body Politick.
Sir *Jerome* in Folio swore by the Mass
This Fart was enough to have blown a Glas:
Quoth then Sir *Jerome* the Lesser, such an Abuse
Was never offer'd in *Poland* nor *Pruce.*[37]

Religio-Moral Satire

Scatological writings in the third group engage in religio-moral satire involving three main topics: antagonists of the English church, greed, and pride. Scatological satire on the antagonists of the church is worth noting for its use of scatology as a device for discrediting or denouncing various adversaries of the church and for its treatment of certain commonplace objects of religious satire, such as the devil, friars, and sin. It illustrates in part Milton's apologia for the use of offensive language on behalf of a just cause, in treating "any notorious enimie to truth."[38]

Harington resorts to scatology as a device for discrediting pagan worship. He selects the two Roman deities associated with the sewer and manure as representatives of pagan worship and ridicules these deities while asserting the superiority of his religion.

> The Romanes euer counted superstitious
> Adored with high titles of Diuinitie,
> Dame *Cloacina,* and the Lord *Sterquitius,*
> Two persons in their State of great affinitie.
> But we, that scorne opinions so pernitious,
> Are taught by Truth well try'd, t'adore the Trinitie.
> And, who-so care of true Religion takes,
> Will think such Saints wel shrined in AIAX.[39]

The scatological wit here is of a crude sort, but the point to note is that, in defense of his church, the author unhesitatingly employs the foulest figures of speech, choosing them deliberately as a device of degradation.[40]

Exploiters of church property suffer a scatological comparison to the devil in another of Harington's satirical epigrams, "Against Church-robbers, vpon a picture that hangs where it is worthy." This epigram lacks the characteristic tight unity of theme typical of most epigrams. Instead, it satirizes the devil, friars, soldiers, court minions, and exploiters of church property. It merits our attention, however, because it satirizes all these subjects in scatological terms.

> The Germans haue a by-word at this houre,
> By *Luther* taught, by Painters skill exprest,
> How Sathan daily Fryers doth deuoure,

Whom in short space he doth so well digest,
That passing downe through his posterior parts,
Tall souldiers thence he to the world deliuers,
And out they flie, all arm'd with pikes and darts,
With halberts, & with muskets and caliuers.
According to these *Lutheran* opinions,
They that deuoure whole Churches and their rents,
I meane our fauorites and Courtly Minions,
Void Forts and Castles, in their excrements.[41]

The epigram is interesting in its treatment of certain commonplace notions: excrement as metaphor for sin, the association of friars with the devil, the devil's excretion as an act of disseminating troubles, the devil as the source of human woes and sins. It satirizes the church robbers (the "fauorites and Courtly Minions") by relating them to satanical acts of devouring and voiding.[42]

Priests also become the object of scatological satire.[43] Some authors make fun of priests for their Roman religion,[44] others for their greed.[45] Most of these satires are humorous scoffings. The notable exception is John Oldham's *Character of a certain Ugly P–* (1684).[46] Compared with this, Oldham's verse satires on Jesuits are tame indeed. The *Character* is instructive because it is one of the most ferocious scatological execrations we have in the language; it shows us to what extreme scatology can be employed. Even in the opening, the mood is contemptuous: "No wonder if I am at a Loss to describe him, whom *Nature* was as much puzzled to make" (p. 325). There are of course degrees of contempt. The contempt here is of the nastiest and most extreme kind. Oldham concentrates on the personal appearance of his victim with grossest exaggeration and in the vilest scatological imagery as though to assert that appearance reflects reality in this case. "I could call him *Nature's Bye-Blow, Miscarriage* and *Abortive* . . ." he says, but declares that "that is stale and flat, and I must flye a higher Pitch to reach his *Deformity*" (p. 325). With this declaration he flings dirt at his hapless victim. Few authors wrote in a more scurrilous vein than he. The portrait he paints is daubed with dirt:

His damn'd squeezing *Close-stool-Face* can be liken'd to nothing better than the *Buttocks* of an old wrinkled *Baboon,* straining upon an *Hillock.* The very *Sight* of him in a Morning would work with one beyond *Jalap* and *Rhubarb.* A *Doctor* (I'm told) once prescrib'd him to one of his *Parishioners* for a *Purge:* he wrought the *Effect,* and gave the *Patient* fourteen *Stools.* 'Tis pity he is not drawn at the *City Charges,* and hung up in some publick *Forica* as a *Remedy* against *Costiveness.*

Indeed, by his *Hue* you might think he had been employed to that use: One would take him for the Picture of *Scoggin* or *Tarleton* on a *Privy-house* Door, which by long standing there has contracted the *Colour* of the neighbouring *Excrements.* Reading lately how *Garagantua* came into the *World* at his Mother's *Ear,* it put an unlucky Thought into my Head concerning him: I presently fancied that he was voided, not brought forth, that his *Dam* was deliver'd of him on t'other side, beshit him coming out, and he has ever since retain'd the *Stains.*

(pp. 326-27)

Reading such a dirty attack as this, we wonder how anyone, let alone any priest, came to deserve such treatment. It seems that this particular priest was guilty of bad preaching. He does not treat the text of his sermon as a whole; he "tear[s] it asunder" (p. 327). He does not interpret the text in a learned manner; "His very *Discourse* stinks in a *Literal Sense;* 'tis *breaking-Wind,* and you'd think he talk'd at the other *End*" (p. 328). His preaching is apparently so bad that the author declares that "*Balaam's* Ass was a better *Divine,* and had a better *Delivery*" and that "He speaks not, but grunts, like one of the *Gadarene Hogs* after the *Devils* enter'd" (p. 333). What is more, he does not merely grunt, but shouts, so loudly that "He has preached half his *Parish* deaf . . ." (p. 333).

Granted that exaggeration is a conventional satiric device, granted also that scatology is a conventional device of ridicule, we nonetheless wonder what sort of satire this is. The specific faults on which the author bases his diatribe do not seem to be grave enough to merit such a merciless onslaught. The scatological description passes the point of recognizable portrait; it becomes grotesque. For our purposes, however, this will prove to be a useful model of comparison. We will recall this work in examining the scatological works of Swift.

The second main topic in religio-moral satire is greed. The scatological denunciation of greed is directed at its two chief manifestations: gluttony and avarice. Both are sins of inordinate appetite and are signs of moral and physical degradation approaching the condition of beasts which have no capacity for reason, therefore, no restraint. Gascoigne's description of gluttony in *The Droome of Doomes Day* (1576) includes the scatological passage in which he declares that "Gluttony dothe rayse a great trybute, but it rendreth a most vyle revenewe. For the more delicate that the meats bee, so much the more styncking are the excrements, and ordure made thereof. He shal doo the more beastly in all things, which doth most greedely loade and powre in. He shal break unsavory and loathsome wynd, bothe upwardes and downwardes, and make an abhominable smell and noyse therewith."[47]

Gluttony is denounced vehemently and vividly through the scatological condemnation of drunkenness. Phineas Fletcher in *The Purple Island* (1633) denounces drunkenness as "insatiate sink" and "thou loathsome putrid swine," and describes it in imagery of vomiting, belching, stinking (VII. 77-78). Among the scatological condemnations of this vice, Richard Young's *The Drunkard's Character* (1638) contains particularly strong passages written to disgust and nauseate the audience in the hope of restraining them from the loathsome vice. The figure of the filthy beast and the scatological imagery used to portray it are commonly employed, but time and again, as in Young's passage below, they engender in the audience disgust and nausea without diminishing the force or vividness by overuse. Young assures the audience that

> the neerest to him [the drunkard] is the *Ierff*, a *beast* in the north parts of *Suetia*, whose *property* (as *Gesner*, out of *Olaus Magnus*, relates it) is when he hath *killed* his *prey*, or found some Carkasse, to fal a *devouring* the same, and never leave *feeding*

> untill his belly be *puft up* . . . and then not being able to hold any more, he goeth presently betweene *two narrow trees* and *straineth* out backward what hee hath eaten, and so being made empty, *returneth* againe to the Carkasse, and filleth himselfe as before, and then straineth it out the second time, and so *continueth filling* and *emptying* himselfe untill he hath *devoured* all; which being consumed, he hunteth after more, and this is the *course* of his *whole life*. Now if the *drunkard*, whose whole life is little els but a *vicissitude* of *devouring* and *vomitting*, who spends all his time in *drinking*, and *venting*, and *abominable spewing*, so disgorging himselfe when he hath drunke his fil, thereby to be able to drinke the like quantity againe, had but this ill quality and not *an hundred more* and *worse* with it, I might well *couple* these two beasts together; for in this particular there cannot be devised a more *expressive Hieroglyphique* of his *loathly condition:* but alas, this is rather one of the drunkards *vertues*, for which he lookes to be *applauded*, and is so by all that keepe him *company*, so that this comparison falls short by much.
>
> (pp. 5-6)

The tone throughout his lengthy treatise is serious, and he employs scatology as a didactic device to produce maximum nausea and disgust.[48]

Avarice is the other chief manifestation of greed and the object of some harsh scatological attack. The attack clearly suggests a carryover from the classical and medieval habit of comparing money to excrement. Juvenal, for instance, uses the term "filthy lucre" ("obscaena pecunia," VI. 298).[49] We find a similar term in Chaucer, "foule usure and lucre of vileyne,/ Hateful to Crist and his companignye" (*The Prioress's Tale*, ll. 491-92).[50] There are numerous later examples of this kind. John Davies of Hereford condemns a young man who weds an old widow for money as having married her "for mucke."[51] The comparison of money to excrement receives pointed expression in Richard Flecknoe's denunciation of the miserly.

Who wholly spends his life in getting wealth,
And to increase his store, consumes himself;
To me does verier Fool than him appear,
Who sold his Horse, to buy him Provender.
Money's like Muck that's profitable, while
'Tis spred abroad, and does inrich a Soyl.
But when 'tis heap'd and hoarded up, methinks
'Tis like a *Dunghil* that lies still and stinks.
And as the Misers treasure does, just so
The Misers self and Memory will do.[52]

We shall see that this old scatological metaphor of money appears again later in certain satires of the eighteenth century. If we do not know this particular tradition, we may find such satire unnecessarily excremental.

The third main topic of religio-moral satire is pride. Since pride stems from man's exaggerated view of his own importance and superiority, scatology is one of the most effective devices for shattering man's hubris. The satirist confronts pride through two basic commonplace ideas. One is the medieval idea of *contemptus mundi* through which he stresses the lowly place of man and his earth in the theocentric perspective of the world; the other is the mortal and animal nature of man.

The idea of *contemptus mundi* is based on the medieval view of human life as justified solely by man's reunion with his creator in the other world. Inasmuch as the other world is glorious and permanent, this world is base and impermanent. In the following epigram, "A Muck-Worme," by John Owen, this concept is stressed through scatology, an ideal metaphor to express something base and contemptible:

Heau'n still views thee, and thou shouldst it still view,
God gaue Heau'n lights, and hath giu'n eyes to you:
Thou canst at once little of this earth see,
But with one turne, halfe Heau'n obseru'd may bee.
Since Heau'n is louely, why lou'st thou Earth rather?
Wantons doe loue their Mam more then the father.[53]

To be sure, in the denotative sense there is nothing scatological in these lines. When juxtaposed with the title, however, the poem takes on scatological implications. For the title establishes the central metaphor of man as a muckworm. In the context of this metaphor, the earth (man's abode) by metaphorical association is seen as a dunghill (the worm's abode). The third and fourth lines give further meaning to these metaphors. The "thou" in the poem can "at once" see "little of this earth," very much like the worm that clings to the dirt so closely that it can see its earth, but only a small part of it. "But with one turne, halfe Heau'n obseru'd may bee." Through the implicit scatological metaphor, the poet seeks to stress the inferior state of this world, to free man from preoccupation with it, and to redirect his vision to heaven.[54]

In crushing human pride, scatology also serves as a powerful reminder of man's base nature. Gascoigne in *The Droome of Doomes Day* details the base nature of man's flesh, asserting that "Man is formed and made of Dust, Clay, Asshes, and a matter much vyler, which for modestie I doe not name . . ." (p. 217), and that after death he becomes "foode of worms, which ever gnaw and feede upon him, & the continewall masse of corruption which alwayes stinketh, & is filthie, odious, and horrible" (p. 218). Then citing man's animal functions, he drags man to the level of odious beasts, lower and more despicable than even the trees and plants:

> O vile unworthinesse of mans estate and condicion, & O unworthy estate of mans vilenesse. Search the trees & the herbes of the Earth, they bringe forth boughes, leaves, flowers, & fruits. A man bringeth forth nitts, lyse & worms. They distill & powre out, Oyle, Wyne, and Balmes, and a man maketh excrements of spettle, pisse, and ordure. They smell & breathe all swetenesse of smell and pleasauntnesse, whereas man belcheth, breaketh wynde and stincketh. . . .
>
> (p. 221)

These are poetic exaggerations of the animal nature of man, but they retain an element of truth that no man can deny, because they are based on facts of human nature and existence. The satirist stresses this commonplace idea through loathsome facts lest man forget them and become proud toward his creator or his fellowmen.[55] If man is such a transitory, vile creature, blasphemy is a damnable sin[56] and arrogance toward his fellowmen absurd. By reducing humanity to a scatological metaphor, the satirist seeks to instill in man a world view based on the theocentric rather than homocentric perspective. His ultimate aim is to deflate man's false sense of his own importance and superiority. In light of this metaphor, the proposition that man is man becomes a meaningful tautology. The following jest, "An answer from a Jaques-Farmer," illustrates this point definitively:

> Divers Gentlemen walking the streets somewhat late, where the Gold-finders were at worke, Fie fellows, say they, what a beastly stinck doe you make? To whom one of the most ancient amongst them replied. If Gentlemen, you, or such as you, keepe your tailes stopped, *You should not now need for to stop your noses.*[57]

Intellectual Satire

Scatological examples in the fourth group belong to what we may call intellectual satire; that is, they denounce certain intellectual vices. These include vices of mind and language, having to do with dull wit and abuses of language, respectively.

Wit, to some authors, is the most distinguishing mark of the civilized man. To them, dull wit or absence of wit is a fact contemptible enough to merit strong ridicule. Thomas Bastard snickers at a dull wit through an image of wetting the mind, in contrast to the "dry beame" of the fine mind:

> A dry beame feedes the mind, as *Pyndar* writes,
> And quickneth reason with refined spirits.
> But your conceipt is dull and nothing such,
> *Lalus;* I think you wett your mind too much.[58]

The image of wetting does not exclude the association of urinating here. The degree of dullness is suggested through the intensifier "too much."

Thomas Wroth develops a scatological metaphor explicitly. A witless brain is equated to excrement—odious, useless—therefore contemptible.

> Litoris holds him for a simple swaine,
> That get's not forty pounds a yeare by's wits;
> But he (me thinks) makes small vse of his braine,
> His shifts are bad, nor dainty are his bits;
> Yet those, to whom the man is better knowne,
> Affirme he vseth all he hath, that's ———.[59]

This kind of scatological metaphor for ill wit is rich in connotation. A filthy or dirty head usually denotes, besides the physical grime, moral and intellectual pollution, suggesting the odiousness of a person's thought and language capable of disgusting and even infecting others. Such a head is often pictured as a fountain of intellectual stagnation and corruption. Nothing can disguise its vileness, poets suggest, not even fine attire. Hence, ill wit is a despicable thing, and poets accordingly deride it.

If ill wit, the source of ill thoughts, arouses poets' derision, ill language, the transmitter of ill wit, deservedly shares the censure. The abuses of language include flattery, detraction, libel, and railing. Guilpin, for example, exposes the odious and hollow nature of railing through a colic simile. The scornful tone is particularly effective in shattering the common association of threat and rage with the pride and impatience of man.

> (Good Lord) that men should haue such kennel wits
> To thinke so well of a scald railing vaine,
> Which soone is vented in beslauered writs.
> As when the cholicke in the gutts doth straine,
> With ciuill conflicts in the same embrac't,
> But let a fart, and then the worst is past.[60]

The prevailing image of the railing fellow is comic as well as squalid.

The man is referred to as a "scald," a scurvy, contemptible fellow. His railing is "vain," soon turned into senseless utterances, suggesting not only foolish talk but also offensive language, spit out in anger.[61] The poet suggests that this railing amounts to nothing more than ridding himself of his vile verbal trash. This "venting" image is further reinforced through the repetition of the same idea in the second half of the poem where the colic simile registers the poet's mounting contempt. The poet implies that one should simply endure such a scene as one must a foul wind; the fellow is really harmless once he has finished his outburst, which eases him. The poet's contempt of the men who admire the railing fellow is perhaps greater than his scorn of the fellow himself. The term "kennel wits," which he employs in referring to the admirers, means "muddy brains." The use of "muddy" here refers to the gutter ("cannel").[62]

If bad speech deserves scatological ridicule, inferior writing, because it is permanently set down on paper, suffers even harsher scatological condemnation. Nashe's *Pierce Penilesse his Supplication to the Diuell* (1592) contains a notable passage of denunciation against inferior writing. In his "Describing the ouer-spreading of *Vice*," Nashe includes an attack on literary trash, "purgations and vomits wrapt vppe in wast paper," turned out by hacks and second-rate authors. His metaphor for such works is considerably harsher than Catullus' *cacata charta* (Poem XXXVI). In bold language and a tone characteristic of Nashe's energetic satires, Pierce Penilesse declares:

> Looke to it, you Booksellers and Stationers, and let not your shops be infected with any such goose gyblets or stinking garbadge, as the Iygs of newsmongers, and especiallie such of you as frequent Westminster hall, let them be circumspect what dunghill papers they bring thither: for one bad pamphlet is enough to raise a damp that may poison a whole Tearme, or at the least a number of poore Clyents, that haue no money to preuent ill aire by breaking their fasts ere they come thither. Not a base Inck-dropper, or scuruy plodder at *Nouerint,* but nailes his asses eares on euerie post, and comes off with long *Circumquaque* to the Gentlemen

> Readers, yea, the most excrementorie dishlickers of learning are growne so valiant in impudencie, that now they set vp their faces (like Turks) of gray paper, to be spet at for siluer games in Finsburie fields.[63]

The degree of exaggeration or accuracy in these comments is not so important here as the tradition of scatological satire in denouncing the alleged abuses of language and inferior writing.[64]

We can see manifestations of this tradition in later examples of intellectual satire as well, notably in Pope's *Dunciad* (1743). As with most other works with scatological elements, *The Dunciad*, too, has been criticized for these elements, usually without any serious attempt to see their thematic relevance to the work.[65] But if we examine the scatological details in Book II with any knowledge of the tradition of scatological satire, we cannot simply dismiss or denounce these elements or the poem on the grounds that scatology as such is bad or serves no literary or artistic purposes whatsoever. And as with most scatological satires, we discover, upon examination, that the scatological details in Book II of *The Dunciad* serve the thematic purposes of the poem effectively.

The poem concludes with the restoration of the Empire of Dulness and the breakdown of social order. "*Religion* blushing veils her sacred fires,/ And unawares Morality expires" (IV. 649-50).[66] The triumph of the dunces is all the more lamentable because they are a contemptible tribe, as well as ridiculous. If the tone is intellectually pessimistic, the mood is bitingly satiric. Pope succeeds in creating this mood through the scatological treatment of the dunces in Book II. The satiric uses of scatology are evident in the kind of "high heroic Games" (II. 18) the dunces carry on. Some participate in a urinary contest in full view of the gaping crowd of dunces "From drawing rooms, from colleges, from garrets" (II. 28). During the footrace, one of the contenders slips into a pile of excrement, offers a prayer to Cloacina for her divine help, and eventually wins the race, revived by the odor of the excrement (II. 69-108).

The diving contest in the same poem is filthier and more topically satirical. The participants dive into the Fleet-ditch mud, which we should recall is no ordinary mud. It is filthy mud, mixed not only with "the large tribute of dead dogs" (II. 272) but also, as we can easily imagine, the contents of chamberpots daily emptied into the ditches. Here Pope utilizes the conventional metaphor of excrement and excremental mud to attack libel and inferior writing as a part of his device for satire. The participants in this contest include, as identified in the argument of the poem, the "dark, and dirty Party-writers" (l.14). At the scene of the contest, the Goddess of Dulness commands the pamphleteers:

> Here prove who best can dash thro' thick and thin,
> And who the most in love of dirt excel
> Or dark dexterity of groping well.
>
> (II. 276-78)

Pope, in a footnote, explains that these are "the three chief qualifications of Party-writers; to stick at nothing, to delight in flinging dirt, and to slander in the dark by guess."[67] Their diving into the mud also suggests "the depths of nastiness to which they will descend" in slandering people.[68] Far from being pointlessly obscene, these passages are painful stings of satire rendered in a conventional metaphor that reveals the odious nature of immoral, unprincipled wielders of destructive pens.

The satire on these literary dunces obviously serves a thematic function. The attacks on these dunces are waged in scatological metaphor, which represents an attack on those authors who thrive because of their immoral writings. The metaphor suggests the general breakdown in the social order, of which literature is an important part.[69] It also provides a violent contrast to the ideal of social order. The contrast involves the two widely different segments of society—the crude world of the urban mass and the cultured world of polite people, the sons of the "Smithfield Muses" and the "Kings" (II. 2). The sons of the Smithfield Muses are anything but the *honnêtes hommes* they seek to replace in all important places of society. They are "the precise opposite of all that is implied by the term 'humanist' or 'enlightened.'"[70]

The restoration of their empire is the breakdown of social order. Progress of dullness is an intellectual, cultural, and moral retrogression. Pope stresses the tragedy of such progress by showing us what sort of beings these dunces are. He succeeds in parading them before us so that we may see for ourselves that they are an immoral, ridiculous, contemptible lot. Through scatology Pope emphasizes their vulgarity and reduces them to the level of dirt-loving brutes, who speak (as Mallarmé would say) "the dialect of the tribe."

We would be wrong to condemn Pope for loving dirt; *he* is condemning those who do.[71] We should remember that *The Dunciad* is not an isolated example of scatological work written by a filthy-minded man. Behind it looms the *Divine Comedy* and the whole tradition of scatological satire. In a sense, Pope's method of satire in Book II is quite Dantesque in having the dunces act out the very activities they themselves indulge in, just as Dante punishes the sinners by forcing them to relive the evils they committed on earth.

By way of concluding this chapter—scatology is a legitimate literary device. Its two main uses are the non-satirical for laughter and the satirical for satire and serious themes. We have seen that scatological humor is a popular genre with a tradition that goes back to the medieval jests. We have also seen that scatology as such does not make a work bad in either a moral or a literary sense. The factors that determine the character and control the effectiveness of scatology in a given work are the author's thematic or artistic purposes and his literary skill. The more skillful the author, the more effectively he will employ this device for his particular purpose, because scatology—like any other literary device—is neutral. If one insists on making a moral judgment of a work with scatological elements, he needs to look at the thematic purpose for which the scatology is employed. Only if the device is employed to evoke laughter by flagrant and pointless reference to excrement, may he judge the work merely filthy or bad.

We may also observe that scatological writings, both non-satirical and satirical, comprise only a small (though distinct) portion of humorous and satirical writings as a whole. In any collection of poems or jests, the proportion of scatological pieces is negligible. This small body of scatological writings, however, constitutes a literary tradition that establishes scatology as a legitimate literary device for both non-satirical and satirical purposes. It remains for us to see for what purposes and with how much skill Swift employs this device.

3

Swift's Scatological Writings (Exclusive of *Gulliver's Travels*)

NON-SATIRICAL USES OF SCATOLOGY

Viewed in the context of literary tradition, Swift uses scatology almost always for satire. Even on occasion, as in the Celia poems, when he tends toward excess in his use of scatology, his basic purpose is not sensationalism but emphasis on the satiric or moral point he is making. Another characteristic of his scatological writings is the intermingling of the satiric and the humorous. If we tend to remember mainly the dark satire and overlook the undercurrent of humor in his scatological writings, we should note that in the latter the tone, for instance, is not always wholly one of anger or attack but, through intermingling of the satiric and the humorous, often ironic. It is a popular misconception to charge Swift with the angriest kind of satire devoid of humor; it is likewise a misconception to charge him with obscenity.

If we single out works that are primarily scatological humor rather than satire, we find only two poems, the verse-riddles "Because I am by Nature blind" (1724?) and "The Gulph of all human Possessions" (1724). Though these belong to the genre of scatological humor, they are not, like some of the stercoraceous jests we have seen, indiscriminately scatological. In this sense none of Swift's scatological writings is stercoraceous—that is, non-satirical in the cloacal tradition of crude jests in which the display of excrement is the source of laughter. Two prose pieces, *The Wonderful Wonder of Wonders* (1720) and *An Examination of Certain Abuses, Corruptions, and Enormities, in the City of Dublin* (1732), may at first appear to be mainly non-satirical, but upon close reading we can see sharp points of satire cunningly hidden beneath the seemingly stercoraceous surface. *The Wonderful Wonder* is outwardly a scatological riddle, but it is at the same time a scatological satire on the proposed National Bank of Ireland. Even the excessively excremental passage in *An Examination of Certain Abuses* is not without stinging satire. I shall examine both of these pieces under socio-political satire.

The verse-riddle on posteriors, "Because I am by Nature blind," is primarily simply humorous and as such is a rare exception in Swift's scatological writings. The humor of the riddle, however, depends not on pointless uses of scatology for its own sake, but on witty uses. The riddle would be crude and even stercoraceous if it depended on indiscriminate references to our anality, but it is characterized by the playfulness of Swift's wit. The opening stanza shows his playful wit at its best:

> Because I am by Nature *blind,*
> I wisely chuse to walk *behind;*
> However, to avoid Disgrace,
> I let no Creature see my *Face.*
> My *Words* are few, but spoke with *Sense:*
> And yet my *speaking* gives Offence:
> Or, if to *whisper* I presume,
> The Company will fly the Room.
> By all the World I am *oppress't,*
> And my *Oppression* gives them *Rest.*[1]

This stanza may be quoted as a complete riddle by itself, and it would be a humorous, though a fairly conventional, riddle on posteriors. The personification of posteriors and related matters—posteriors as face and flatulency as an act of speaking—are conventional figures that appear in various writings. We have seen that the transformed body of the sorcerer in Dante's *Inferno* (XX.22-24) carries its face on its posteriors (in this case to signify the odiousness and devilishness of the sorcery). In Chaucer's *The Miller's Tale,* when Absolon kisses Alison's "ers" by mistake, he thinks of her face and is at first bewildered by its hair. The second time, expecting the same prank, he seeks for her arse by asking, "Spek, sweete bryd, I noot nat where thou art," whereupon Nicholas "anon leet fle a fart" and meets his disaster. Of the half-dozen scatological riddles included in *The Demaundes Joyous* (1511), there is one that reads: "Demaunde. Who was he that lete the fyrst farte at rome. That was the arse" (p.3).

The following riddle on a fart in *Thesaurus Aenigmaticus* (1725-26) makes a good comparison to Swift's stanza above, especially since it is of the same length and on a similar topic.

> To all round me Mirth I make, tho seldom spend
> my Pelf;
> And whatso'ere I chance to say, I always shame my self.
> I'm usher'd into Company of those of best Degree,
> Who all congratulating Bow, when 'ere they know 'tis me.
> Yet whoso'ere me entertains, turns usually a Sneaker,
> Tho' of the Commons House ('tis true) I once was Mr.
> Speaker.
> And tho I'm chose no Member now, I often fill the Chair
> But very seldom come into't if th' Speaker be not there.
> I live to so great length of Age, I die for want of Breath,
> And yet when'ere I hap to die, I sing before my Death.
>
> (p. 35)

Both Swift's stanza and this anonymous riddle are playful in their extended uses of personification of arse and of puns on the various meanings of the verb "speak" (to communicate through voicing "natural" words; to express one's opinion; to make one's presence known; to fart).

Without going into a detailed discussion, we may generally observe that Swift's riddle is more polished in its neat, compact phrasing, more playful in its puns ("spoke with *Sense*"; "if to *whisper* I presume"; "my

Oppression gives them *Rest*") and wittier in its rhyme ("blind/behind"; "Disgrace/Face"; "Sense/Offence"; "oppress't/Rest"). Had Swift's riddle stopped at the end of the first stanza, it would still be a superior example of scatological humor based on the conventional conceit of "face-arse." But characteristically Swift extends this basic conceit by mingling with it two unexpected conceits of "money-excrements" and "Bank-posteriors" (which will be instructive for us to recall in our discussion of *The Wonderful Wonder*, the satire on the Bank). The financial imagery breaks into the poem in the second stanza.

> By Thousands I am *sold* and *bought*,
> Who neither get, nor lose a Groat;
> For none, alas, by me can gain,
> By those who give me *greatest Pain*.
> (ll.13-16)

That this refers to the act of natural necessity becomes apparent when we appreciate the clever play on "sold" and "bought." The various meanings of "sell" listed in *NED* include "to hand over (something, esp. food, a gift) voluntarily or in response to a demand; to give up or part with one thing in exchange for another." "Buy" means, among other things, "to obtain . . . in exchange for something else, or by making some sacrifice; to set free by paying a price." The conceits of "money-excrements" and "Bank-posteriors" become clear in the last stanza of the poem, part of which is quoted below.

> In me, Detractors seek to find
> Two Vices of a diff'rent Kind:
> I'm too *profuse* some Cens'rers cry,
> And all I get, I *let it fly*:
> While others give me many a Curse,
> Because too *close* I hold my *Purse*.
> (ll.23-28)

In the closing lines of the riddle, the jocular reference to the anality of the personified posteriors with which the poem began continues with the final imagery:

I'm always by my Betters led;
I last *get up*, am first *a-bed*;
Though, if I rise *before my Time*,
The Learn'd in Sciences sublime,
Consult the Stars, and thence foretell
Good Luck to those with whom I dwell.
(ll.39-44)

The other piece, "The Gulph of all human Possessions," is a riddle on a privy. Though this is much more heavily scatological, Swift no more indulges in scatology for its own sake than in "Because I am by Nature blind." The total effect of the poem is one of humor and satire, humor somewhat tipping the balance. While humor burlesques a privy as well as certain traditional philosophical ideas, satire emerges from the good-humored, if gross, moral implications concerning human life.

The mock-heroic setting (Olympus and "Jove . . . among the Gods," ll. 95-96) and the parody on epic style provoke humor from the beginning. Pointing at a public privy as a visible symbol of the vanity of human wishes, Jove talks to mortal mankind ("Vain Man") about the human condition in a tone partly humorous in its mock-heroic diction and partly satirical in the contemptuous imperative of the opening lines.

Come hither and behold the Fruits,
Vain Man, of all thy vain Pursuits.
Take wise Advice, and *look behind*,
Bring all *past* Actions to thy Mind.
Here you may see, as in a Glass,
How soon all human Pleasures pass.
How will it mortify thy Pride,
To turn the true impartial Side!
How will your Eyes contain their Tears,
When all the sad *Reverse* appears![2]

The element of satire is discernible in the slight jeering emphasis on man's animal nature and the vanity of mortal man's feverish struggle for personal gain. Swift refers to morally corrupt men in particular, as though he were implying that good men seldom achieve material prosperity. He sees successful men as vain and proud, and the gains they make as foul. The word "Designs" in the following passage suggests clever schemes, evil policy, and calculated actions of ambitious men bent on acquiring profit.

> This Cave within its Womb confines
> The last Result of all Designs:
> Here lye deposited the Spoils
> Of busy Mortals endless Toils:
> Here, with an easy Search we find
> The *foul Corruptions* of Mankind.
> The wretched Purchase here behold
> Of Traytors who their Country sold.
>
> This Gulph insatiable imbibes
> The Lawyer's Fees, the Statesman's Bribes.
> Here, in their proper Shape and Mein,
> Fraud, Perjury, and Guilt are seen.
>
> (ll. 11-22)

The emphasis on our anality, as in the following passage, is so scatological in its humor that some may find it excessively excremental. But here again, scatology is not used pointlessly or as a needless reminder of our animal nature. It touches on a recurring theme of Swift's scatological writings—the absurdity of our affecting superior social status. Excrement serves as a common denominator for all living men of whatever social class or origin.

> Necessity, the Tyrant's Law,
> All human Race must hither draw:
> All prompted by the same *Desire,*
> The vig'rous Youth, and aged Sire:
> Behold, the Coward, and the Brave,
> The haughty Prince, the humble Slave,
> Physician, Lawyer, and Divine,

All make *Oblations* at this Shrine.
Some enter boldly, some by Stealth,
And leave *behind* their fruitless Wealth.
For, while the bashful Sylvan Maid,
As half asham'd, and half afraid,
Approaching, finds it hard to part
With that which dwelt so *near her Heart;*
The courtly Dame, unmov'd by Fear,
Profusely pours her *Off'rings* here.[3]

Though Maurice Johnson does not discuss either of these two riddles in his study of Swift's poems, his general comment on excrement as a symbol applies here when he asserts that excrement in Swift's poems is "a symbol which perhaps better than any other reduces all mankind to a single level."[4] We may add that this downward movement is a levelling to the lowest common rung. While the implications of this downward pull are moral, they are also humorous, especially when we compare this passage with the graveyard scene in *Hamlet* (V.i) where the implications of Hamlet's comments on the insignificance of human ambition and rank are more grim, because death levels all men to dust and food for worms. Swift, on the other hand, capitalizes on our sense of shame concerning our animal nature and the gross necessities we share with all living men, if not all living things.

Swift concludes the riddle by reminding us of man's close relationship to lowly things by burlesquing the traditional philosophical idea of the organic cyle of nature (the pattern of birth, growth, decay, death, and rebirth, the unity and interrelationship of all things).

Yet from this *mingled Mass* of Things,
In Time a new Creation springs.
These *crude* Materials once shall rise,
To fill the Earth, and Air, and Skies:
In various Forms appear agen
Of Vegetables, Brutes, and Men.[5]

Regardless of our social status and whether we like it or not, we are all cohabitants of this earthly community in a mutually connected, symbiotic relationship with everything else in it, including "These *crude* Materials." This reminder serves as an antidote to our pride and affectation.

We can now see that despite its heavier scatological humor, this poem is not a simple literary *jeu d'esprit*. The riddle on a privy with its mixed humor reminds us of Erasmus' comment on literary trifles. In his dedicatory epistle to Thomas More, Erasmus defends his "trifle," *The Praise of Folly* (1509), on the authority of literary precedents, including those by Homer and Vergil. He then observes, "How unjust it is, when all other ways of life are permitted their diversions, that none is allowed to studies. Especially this is true since literary jests may have serious implications, and since a reader with a keen nose may get more from a skilful trifle than from a solemn and stately argument."[6] Neither Erasmus nor More would have accused Swift of pointless obscenity.

In concluding our examination of Swift's non-satirical uses of scatology, we may see how obscene Swift's scatological humor is by comparing it with two examples from other authors. One is by Herrick, "Upon *Skoles*."

> *Skoles* stinks so deadly, that his Breeches loath
> His dampish Buttocks furthermore to cloath:
> Cloy'd they are up with Arse; but hope, one blast
> Will whirle about, and blow them thence at last.[7]

The other is by Richard Middleton of York, "*In Dollabellam*."

> Signior *Pancrates* in his sapience,
> Saith this word Pulchritude is no eloquence.
> Now to approue my rime in making verses,
> A tale of *Dollabella* he rehearses.
> He saith *Dollabella* is so big,
> And so imbost with fat of swine and pig,
> That he cannot with hands superiors
> Remove the excrements from his posteriors.
> Therefore *Pancrates* said, this fat grosse hog

Is still associate with a little dog;
Who, when his master walkes to Aiax seat
T'auoid the superfluity of his meat,
Duely attends, (said he,) and is so kinde,
Lickes with his tongue the excrements behinde;
But if his dogge be absent, what is then?
He will not call his maides or seruingmen
To spunge the place; but (in a cunning kind)
A stake hard by the priuie you shall finde,
Couered with cloth, standing some halfe yeard high,
Whereon he purges his concauity:
And stooping downe towards the stifned stake,
With cloth thereon, his taile he cleane doth make.
This did *Pancrates* say, then blame not me,
I made but th' rime, let him the author be.[8]

These are extreme examples, but it is through such examples that we can better understand the character of Swift's scatological humor and weigh the charge of obscenity made against Swift. The superiority of the humor in Swift's pieces is surely apparent.

SATIRICAL USES OF SCATOLOGY

When we survey Swift's scatological writings, we can see that he is traditional: he does not experiment with a new literary genre but writes in conventional forms. Thus, his occasional indulgence in scatological humor is not a unique or isolated literary phenomenon. He inherited his scatology as a conventional literary device from many skillful predecessors. Nor is his use of scatology in satire unique and therefore scandalous. To be sure, he uses scatology more often than many other writers, but more effectively. The use therefore becomes one mark of Swift's great skill.

As in the preceding chapter, I will examine Swift's uses of scatology for satirical purposes under four thematic categories: (1) personal satire, (2) socio-political satire, (3) religio-moral satire, and (4) intellectual satire.

Personal Satire

Personal satire, intended to denounce or ridicule specific individuals for personal reasons, does not occupy a prominent place in Swift's scatological writings. Most of his personal satire is written in non-scatological language, for example, the attack against Wotton and Bentley in *The Battle of the Books* (1704).[9] We do not find extended passages of personal invective similar to those exchanged between Nashe and Harvey. When Swift delivers personal satire in scatological language, it is usually against a person who represents or belongs to a particular class or group. In *The Legion Club,* for instance, Swift vilifies specific individuals as members of the Irish House of Commons for their stand on a public issue. (I examine this work under socio-political satire.)

Two notable examples of personal satire are "Clad all in Brown" and "The Problem." Swift does not use the names of the principal persons satirized in either of these poems, but the references presumably are to Richard Tighe and Henry Sidney respectively.[10] In "Clad all in Brown" (1728), Swift parodies "the tenth poem of Cowley's *Mistress,* entitled 'Clad all in White.' "[11] More specifically, it is a skillful travesty of the original in substance as well as a close parody of its form and style. A comparison of the opening couplet in each poem suggests the kind of parody and travesty Swift indulges in. Cowley describes his mistress: "Fairest thing that shines below,/ Why in this robe dost thou appear?" Swift, however, describes something quite different: "Foulest Brute that stinks below,/ Why in this Brown dost thou appear?" We may further compare the second and third stanzas of each poem for a better appreciation of the lively wit in Swift's lampoon. This is Cowley:

'Tis not the linen shows so fair,
Her skin shines thro', and makes it bright;
So, clouds themselves like suns appear,
When the sun pierces them with light;
So, lilies in a glass enclose,
The glass will seem as white as those.

Thou now one heap of beauty art,
Nought outwards, or within, is foul;
Condensed beams make every part;
Thy body's clothed like thy soul—
Thy soul, which does itself display,
Like a star plac'd i' th' Milky-way.[12]

This is Swift:

'Tis not the Coat that looks so dun,
His Hide emits a Foulness out,
Not one Jot better looks the Sun
Seen from behind a dirty Clout:
So T—rds within a Glass inclose,
The Glass will seem as brown as those.

Thou now one Heap of Foulness art,
All outward and within is foul;
Condensed Filth in e'ry Part,
Thy Body's cloathed like thy Soul.
Thy Soul, which through thy Hide of Buff,
Scarce glimmers, like a dying Snuff.
(*Poems*, III, 786-87)

The association of the Brute with excrement is all too clear. In the concluding stanza, Swift depicts this Brute as having "an honest Trade" of collecting "dust" from house to house.[13] The association of excrement with moral corruption is also clear when we recognize the Platonic idea of the relationship between the physical and the spiritual world implicit in the third stanza of Cowley's poem quoted above (e.g., "Thy body's clothed like thy soul," which Swift borrows verbatim) burlesqued by Swift ("All outward and within is foul"); according to this idea, as Spenser asserts in "An Hymne in Honovr of Beavtie" (1596), "For of the soule the bodie forme doth take:/ For soule is forme, and doth the bodie make" (ll.132-33).

"The Problem" (1699), the other example of Swift's personal satire, is a much more scurrilous lampoon. The satire is directed against an unnamed antagonist in the company of three of his mistresses who are named.[14] The object of the satire is to vilify the antagonist known for his lechery by reducing him to the level of the beastial Yahoo that emits, when inflamed with animal heat, "a most offensive Smell." Swift shows the man to be incapable of controlling his ruling passion, unable to rest until his passion is consummated. Swift emphasizes the vile character of the man and the odiousness of his lechery through scatological imagery that pervades the poem.

> Love's Fire, it seems, like inward Heat,
> Works in my Lord by St[oo]l and Sweat,
> Which brings a St–k from ev'ry Pore,
> And from behind, and from before.
> (*Poems*, I, 65, ll. 7-10)

The object of his lust is equally odious, because only ladies of similarly filthy passion may identify his beastial heat: "Yet, what is wonderful to tell it,/ None but the Fav'rite Nymph can smell it" (ll. 11-12). Then, through his wit that reminds us of Donne's in its startling parallels, Swift suggests the beastial and excremental associations of the man's particular kind of lust through the combination of pun on "ass" (beast, stupid person, posteriors) and the conceit of bowstring and bowel movement.

> . . . deep Scholars know,
> That the main String of Cupid's Bow,
> Once on a Time, was an A[sses] Gut,
> Now to a nobler Office put,
> By Favour, or Desert preferr'd
> From giving Passage to a T–.
> But still, tho' fixt among the Stars,
> Does sympathize with Human A–.
> Thus when you feel an hard-bound B–
> Conclude Love's Bow-String at full Stretch;
> Till the kind L[oo]seness comes, and then
> Conclude the Bow relax'd again.
> (ll. 21-32)

The central incident of the poem concerns three ladies and their attempt to gain the favor of the Lord by identifying his lust-smell:

> And now the Ladys all are bent,
> To try the great Experiement;
> Ambitious of a Regent's Heart
> Spread all their Charms to catch a F—;
> Watching the first unsav'ry Wind,
> Some ply before, and some behind.
> My Lord, on Fire amidst the Dames,
> F—s like a Laurel in the Flames.
> The Fair approach the speaking Part,
> To try the Back-way to his Heart;
> For, as when we a Gun discharge,
> Altho' the Bore be ne'er so large,
> Before the Flame from Muzzle burst,
> Just at the Breech it flashes first:
> So from my Lord his Passion broke,
> He f—ted first, and then he spoke.
>
> (ll. 33-48)

The poem ends with each of the ladies claiming to have smelled the scent and proclaiming him, therefore, to be "an universal Lover" (l. 60).[15]

Stylistically there is a wide gap between these lampoons and such earlier examples of personal satire as Skelton's *Poems against Garnesche* (1513-14). While both belong to the same tradition of personal satire, which employs scatology as a device for discrediting, deriding, or demolishing an antagonist, Swift changes this generic function of scatology by satirizing his antagonists through witty lampoon rather than blunt invective. We have seen that Skelton attacks his enemy in a concentrated, extended, and direct denunciation couched in pungent language reminiscent of Nashe's scathing satire against the Harvey brothers and in a tone and mood that recall Juvenalian concentration and intensity. Swift, on the other hand, changes this literary tradition and resorts to wit and humor to effect the personal satire he desires.

While his mood is satiric, his tone is largely witty and humorous. In "The Problem," the satiric mood is evident in the scatological association Swift brings about between the Lord's lechery and his mistresses; the witty and humorous tone is readily identifiable in the conceit of farting "like a Laurel in the Flames" followed by the extended metaphor of the gun and the degradation of the laurel, the crown of fame in classical times, now consumed by flames to produce the rude sound of the simile, which at the same time effects an exact auditory image. We have already seen that the earlier poem, "Clad all in Brown," is also a very witty personal satire. Though it is scatological in its imagery, we must recognize Swift's lively imagination that first saw the applicability of Cowley's poem to his satiric purpose and then carried out the complete reversal of the original. We can then understand Swift's skillful parody of Cowley's style and the travesty he makes of the poem's substance, including the Platonic idea of correspondence. Unlike the earlier examples of Skelton and Nashe, the general effect of Swift's personal satire as seen in these two poems is largely subtle wit, which maintains a humorous tone and a mockingly scornful mood. This element of wit is a peculiarly Swiftian quality that turns personal satire into works of ingenious lampoon as well as mocking personal attack.

Socio-Political Satire

The main examples of socio-political satire in Swift's scatological writings include *The Wonderful Wonder of Wonders* (1720), *An Examination of Certain Abuses, Corruptions, and Enormities in the City of Dublin* (1732), and *A Character, Panegyric, and Description of the Legion Club* (1736). Of these, the first two—both prose pieces—deal with social topics, and the last—a poem—with a political group.

An Examination of Certain Abuses is not primarily a scatological satire, but it contains an excremental passage interesting for its satirical quality. The author begins the pamphlet with a humorous description of some of the "Abuses, Corruptions, and Enormities, in the City of Dublin." He protests, for example, the mendacity of street venders who cry "Herrings alive, alive" in language that betrays his humor:

"And, pray how is it possible, that a *Herring*, which, as *Philosophers* observe, cannot live longer than One Minute, Three Seconds and a half out of Water, should bear a Voyage in open Boats from *Howth* to *Dublin*, be tossed into twenty Hands, and preserve its Life in Sieves for several Hours? Nay, we have Witnesses ready to produce, that many Thousands of these Herrings, so impudently asserted to be alive, have been a Day and a Night upon dry land."[16] The satirical character of the pamphlet emerges, however, in his description of other cries like "Dirt to carry out," which the author cites in reference to party faction and "political Dirt":

> There is a *Cry* peculiar to this City, which I do not remember to have been used in *London;* or at least, not in the same Terms that it hath been practised by both Parties, during each of their Power; but, very unjustly by the *Tories*. While these were at the Helm, they grew daily more and more impatient to put all true *Whigs* and *Hanoverians* out of Employments. To effect which, they hired certain ordinary Fellows, with large Baskets on their Shoulders, to call aloud at every House, *Dirt to carry out;* giving that Denomination to our whole Party; as if they would signify, that the Kingdom could never be *cleansed*, until we were *swept* from the Earth like *Rubbish*. But, since that happy Turn of Times, when we were so *miraculously* preserved by just an *Inch*, from *Popery, Slavery, Massacre,* and the *Pretender;* I must own it Prudence in us, still to go on with the same *Cry;* which hath ever since been so effectually observed, that the true *political Dirt* is wholly removed, and thrown on its proper Dunghills, there to corrupt and be no more heard of.[17]

The excremental passage I referred to earlier, however, is the paragraph that immediately follows the above quotation. In it the author describes, by way of complaint and censure, the shameful condition of Dublin streets littered with human excrement. Though it is heavily scatological, it is nevertheless an interesting passage to note because it illustrates a characteristic technique of Swift's scatological satire—the mingling of the humorous and the satiric.

> Every Person who walks the Streets, must needs observe the immense Number of human Excrements at the Doors and Steps of waste Houses, and at the Sides of every dead Wall; for which the disaffected Party hath assigned a very false and malicious Cause. They would have it that these Heaps were laid there privately by *British Fundaments,* to make the World believe, that our *Irish* Vulgar do daily eat and drink; and consequently, that the Clamour of Poverty among us, must be false; proceeding only from *Jacobites* and *Papists.* They would confirm this, by pretending to observe, that a *British Anus* being more narrowly perforated than one of our own Country; and many of these Excrements, upon a strict View appearing Copple-crowned, with a Point like a Cone or Pyramid, are easily distinguished from the *Hibernian,* which lie much flatter, and with less Continuity. I communicated this Conjecture to an eminent Physician, who is well versed in such profound Speculations; and at my Request was pleased to make Trial with each of his Fingers, by thrusting them into the *Anus* of several Persons of both Nations; and professed he could find no such Difference between them as those ill-disposed People alledge. On the contrary, he assured me, that much the greater Number of narrow Cavities were of *Hibernian* Origin. This I only mention to shew how ready the *Jacobites* are to lay hold of any Handle to express their Malice against the Government. I had almost forgot to add, that my Friend the Physician could, by smelling each Finger, distinguish the *Hibernian* Excrement from the *British;* and was not above twice mistaken in an Hundred Experiments; upon which he intends very soon to publish a learned Dissertation.[18]

To the reader unaccustomed to this kind of medley, this passage may seem merely stercoraceous. To be sure, it is stercoraceous, but as in most of Swift's scatological writings, it is not so pointlessly excremental as it may appear. It denounces the Irish for being barbaric and indifferent to public cleanliness, although Dublin at that time cannot have been too different from London or any other city, except perhaps

Edinburgh.[19] A much more significant reference is made to the British exploitation of Ireland. The reference to the British and the hunger and "the Clamour of Poverty" among the Irish echo the distress and indignation expressed earlier, most memorably in *A Modest Proposal* (1729). While the manner of satire is crudely humorous in its excremental insinuation, the reference to the British exploitation of Ireland points up the sharp edges of painful truth. The passage also makes fun of the Whigs' ready suspicion of Tory Jacobites by imputing to the "disaffected Party" its readiness to cover up a dire economic situation and by charging the Jacobites with being ready "to lay hold of any Handle to express their Malice against the Government."[20]

The Wonderful Wonder, however, is wholly scatological in a humorous manner. It is outwardly a description of posteriors and seems to be entirely non-satirical; in a sense it is an extended riddle on posteriors. The piece concludes, for example, with the following passage that describes but does not identify the subject:

> There is so general an Opinion of his Justice, that sometimes very *hard Cases* are left to his Decision: And while he *sits* upon them, he carries himself exactly *even between both Sides,* except where some *knotty Point* arises; and then he is observed to *lean* a little to the *Right,* or *Left,* as the *Matter* inclines him; his Reasons for it are so manifest and convincing, that every Man approves them.[21]

The satirical elements in this piece are not immediately evident, but they are intended as an attack on the Bank. Herbert Davis points out that "the original London edition of 1721 . . . contains the following additional sentence, of importance because of its reference to the Bank: 'He lives from *Hand* to *Mouth,* but however, the greatest and wisest People will trust him with all their ready Money, which he was never known to *Embezzle,* except, very rarely, when he is sacrificing to his Goddesses below.'"[22] The omission of this sentence in Faulkner's edition of 1735 makes it difficult for us to see at once the satire on the Bank. Even without this important sentence, if we examine the piece carefully in the light of Swift's scatological references to money in other works, we can recognize passages that function doubly as a humorous description of posteriors and a satiric description of the Bank. Not all the passages carry this double meaning; many of them are simply humorous descriptions of posteriors.

Implicit in the satire is the metaphor of excrement for money and gold. In the verse-riddle on posteriors, "Because I am by Nature blind," we noted the financial metaphor of purse for posteriors.[23] We recall this metaphor in *The Wonderful Wonder* when we read that "He has the Reputation to be a *close, griping, squeezing* Fellow; and that when his Bags are *full,* he is often needy; yet, when the Fit takes him, as fast as he gets, he lets it fly" (pp. 281-82). Here the double meaning is obvious when we go on to read that "He hath been constituted by the *higher* Powers in the Station of *Receiver-General;* in which Employment, some have censured him for playing *fast* and *loose.* He is likewise *Overseer* of the *Golden Mines,* which he daily inspects, when his Health will permit him" (p. 282). We may further note that "In *Politicks,* he always submits to what is *uppermost* . . ." and "In him we may observe the true Effects and Consequences of *Tyranny* in a State: For, as he is a great *Oppressor* of all *below* him, so there is no body more *oppressed* by those *above* him: Yet in his Time, he hath been so highly in Favour, that many *illustrious Persons* have been entirely indebted to *him* for their *Preferments*" (p. 283). The satire also contains a sentence that reminds us of the verse-riddle on a privy, "The Gulph of all human Possessions": "He hath discovered from his own Experience the true *Point,* wherein all human Actions, Projects, and Designs do chiefly *terminate;* and how *mean* and *sordid* they are *at the Bottom*" (pp. 283-84).[24]

We can now see more clearly the possibility of the scatological satire on the Bank. The whole piece rests on the metaphor of excrement equaling money. From this basic metaphor we can easily see the reference to "Golden Mines" as the excremental pile and the Bank as the posteriors that discharge these golden mines at a privy. Swift's contemporaries for whom the piece was written seem to have detected this satire easily. *The Blunderful Blunder of Blunders* (1722?), which jests at Swift's satire (it carries the subtitle "Being an Answer to *The Wonderful Wonder of Wonders.* Ars longa."), ends with the postscript that contains the following sentence: "If the *Gentleman,* thro' Consideration of the Losses sustained by the *South-Sea,* has out of a Design to encourage *Trade* and *Commarse,* sold the Publick a Bargain, I heartily ask his Pardon for these Animadversions" (p. 4).[25]

While *An Examination of Certain Abuses* and *The Wonderful Wonders* display the intermingling of the humorous and the satirical, *The Legion Club,* a major example of political satire, is conspicuously devoid of humor. From beginning to end it is a bitter verse-satire against the Irish House of Commons. The kind of scatological satire we see in *The Legion Club* (1736), "the last and bitterest of his satires,"[26] may be seen earlier in "Ode to the King" (1691), one of Swift's earliest writings. The ode is not a satire; it celebrates King William's successful Irish expedition against Louis XIV of France. The concluding section of the poem, however, contains a scatological invective against the French king. The bold use of scatology, even in this early work, is characteristic of Swift's scatological writings. The young author scornfully describes the ignoble downfall of the French monarch. William's foe, the author declares, is one who

> Took its first Growth and Birth
> From the worst Excrements of Earth;[27]
> Stay but a little while and down again 'twill come,
> And end as it began, in Vapour, Stink, and Scum.
> (*Poems,* I, 10, ll. 126-29)

And he concludes the poem with the following description of the French monarch's defeat by William:

> Our Prince has hit Him, like *Achilles,* in the *Heel,*
> The poys'nous Darts has made him reel,
> Giddy he grows, and down is hurl'd,
> And as a Mortal to his *Vile Disease,*[28]
> Falls sick in the *Posteriors* of the World.
> (ll. 142-46)

Scatology is employed more pervasively in *The Legion Club.*[29] Throughout it is a violent lampoon, marked by scatological imagery and harsh condemnation, against the members of the Irish House of Commons. It is directed against the members of the House in general, as well as specific individuals identified by name. Swift considers them a demonic lot—corrupt, evil, and damned; hence, the appellation of the Legion Club with its biblical allusion to the "unclean spirit" and "devils."[30] A glance at the epithets Swift uses for the members suggests the intensity of his rage against them. The satire is strewn with such opprobrious terms as "These Demoniacs" (l. 11), "the Den of Thieves" (l. 28), "that Harpies Nest" (l. 29), "Monkeys" (l. 82), "Hell" (l. 86), "this odious Crew" (l. 93), "Mad-House" (l. 99), "Brutes" (l. 113), "Monster" (l. 222), "this odious Group of Fools" (l. 224), "the Beasts" (l. 225). Some of the terms used against specific individuals include such terrifying names as "Briareus" (l. 103), "Satan" (l. 138), "Gorgon" (l. 194).

Scatological imagery blends into the bristling language of lampoon to make of the House an excremental pandemonium of fools and lunatics reminiscent of Bedlam in *A Tale of a Tub* as well as of the satanic crew in Milton's Hell. In fact, behind this infernal House of Commons looms the Underworld of Homer, Vergil, Dante, and Milton. As indicated by Faulkner's notes to the poem (ll. 83, 87, 91, 93, 97, 103, *Poems* III, 832-33), Swift parodies Aeneas' visit to the underworld in particular and the epic device of a descent into Hades in general. Scatology therefore becomes particularly appropriate to this satire, for the Legion Club almost by definition would then be a place of excremental sight, smell, and discordant noises. The visitor is astounded by the tumultuous assembly:

> Such a Noise, and such haranguing,
> When a Brother Thief is hanging.
> Such a Rout and such a Rabble
> Run to hear Jackpudding gabble;
> Such a Croud their Ordure throws
> On a far less Villain's Nose.
>
> (ll. 15-20)

Clio, the counterpart of the companion and guide whom the epic hero takes with him in order to be safe in his venture into the underworld, is overpowered by the miasma and is forced to turn away:

> Never durst a Muse before
> Enter that Infernal Door;
> *Clio* stifled with the Smell,
> Into Spleen and Vapours fell;
> By the *Stygian* Steams that flew,
> From the dire infectious Crew.
> Not the Stench of Lake *Avernus*,
> Could have more offended her Nose;
> Had she flown but o'er the Top,
> She would feel her Pinions drop,
> And by Exhalations dire,
> Though a Goddess must expire.
> (ll. 119-30)

The passage refers to Avernus, the Birdless Place, of the *Aeneid* (VI. 237-42). While Vergil's Sibyl remains with Aeneas, Swift's Clio "In a Fright . . . crept away" (l. 131), so much worse is this Avernus which is contaminated by an excremental assembly. The olfactory imagery here is also Dantesque—the foul smell is associated with moral corruption and the excremental inferno with vile sinners.

While the scatological aspect of this poem is unmistakable, Swift does not indulge heavily in scatology. Instead, he employs it sporadically as an effective means of defaming the members of the Legion Club. The occasional scatological passages serve as repeated attacks; as an example, in one stanza the scatological line is employed in the main clause as the main stroke, preceded by the subordinate clause.

> While they never hold their Tongue,
> Let them dabble in their Dung;
> . . . .
> We may, while they strain their throats,
> Wipe our A--s with their V--.
> (ll. 51-52, 61-62)

Elsewhere the visitor sarcastically says, "Dear Companions hug and kiss,/ Toast *old Glorious* in your Piss" (ll. 151-52).[31] (Part of the sarcasm lies in the devastating rhyme of "kiss" and "Piss" as in "Tongue" and "Dung" above.)

Swift closes the poem by stressing once more the odiousness of the place and the assembly. When the keeper of the House explains that the visitor has "hardly seen a Score" (l. 237) and volunteers to show "two hundred more" (l. 238), the visitor declines the offer, confessing "But I feel my Spirits spent,/With the Noise, the Sight, the Scent" (ll. 233-34). Casting a last glance at the assembly, the visitor utters his departing curse: "May their God, the Devil confound 'em" (l. 242).

While the scatological poems on the Rump parliament, such as "Upon the Parliament Fart," build their satire on humorous mockery, *The Legion Club* derives its force from the intensity of its satire. This intensity is achieved partly by the tone of the poem, which is one of rage devoid of any humor and partly by the effective use of scatology. Though Swift does not employ scatology heavily, he uses it effectively for lampoon: it is appropriate to the general conception of the House of Commons as an infernal meeting place and its members as demoniacs whose god is the devil.

Religio-Moral Satire

Swift's religio-moral satire includes *A Tale of a Tub* and the notorious Celia poems, works that readers have misunderstood since their original publication. The religious satire in the *Tale* has brought charges of profanity and atheism against Swift, and the moral satire in the Celia poems has brought charges of obscenity and immorality against him. This misunderstanding stems largely from the failure of the reader to appreciate Swift's religious and moral purposes.

The religious satire in the *Tale* is not a satire on religion but on "Abuses" and "Corruptions" in religion. In answer to those critics who charged him with irreverence, Swift states emphatically in "An Apology" added to the fifth edition (1710) of the *Tale,* "Why should any Clergyman of our Church be angry to see the Follies of Fanaticism and Superstition exposed, tho' in the most ridiculous Manner? since that is perhaps the most probable way to cure them, or at least to hinder them from farther spreading" (p. 5).

Swift does employ scatology in attacking certain aspects of religious abuse and corruption. He singles out certain "inventions" of Peter, the Papist brother, as the targets for his scatological ridicule. While scatology is not used heavily, Swift's desire to ridicule and degrade through scatological associations is clear. One of the inventions or "projects" Swift mentions is Peter's "Sovereign Remedy for the *Worms,* especially those in the *Spleen*" (p. 107). A footnote indicates clearly for the benefit of those who might misunderstand the satire that "Here the Author ridicules the Penances of the Church of *Rome,* which may be made as easy to the Sinner as he pleases, provided he will pay for them accordingly." The "Sovereign Remedy" involves a ridiculous treatment, which suggests Swift's contemptuous attitude toward Peter's invention. The image Swift uses to express this contempt is medical, suggestive of quackery and fraud on the part of the healer capitalizing on the gullibility and stupidity of the sick.[32] Among other things, the patient "must also duly confine his two Eyes to the same Object; and by no means break Wind at both Ends together, without manifest Occasion. These Prescriptions diligently observed, the *Worms* would void insensibly by Perspiration, ascending thro' the *Brain*" (p. 107).

Another invention Swift scoffs at is confession. Again the image used is medical and has to do with disorders of the mind and the bowels. This particular invention, Swift describes, is "the Erecting of a *Whispering-Office,* for the Publick Good and Ease of all such as are Hypochondriacal, or troubled with the Cholick; as likewise of all Eves-droppers, Physicians, Midwives, small Politicians, Friends fallen out, Repeating Poets, Lovers Happy or in Despair, Bawds, Privy-Counsellours, Pages, Parasites and Buffoons; In short, of all such as are in Danger of bursting with too much *Wind*" (pp. 107-08). (We might note parenthetically that the various groups of people named do not make up an attractive crowd.) The wind here carries multiple associations, none of them attractive. In the immediate context it suggests flatulency; it also suggests nonsense and tattling. The figure of the confessor and the whole process of confession are no less unattractive and degrading: "An *Asse*'s Head was placed so conveniently, that the Party affected might easily with his Mouth accost either of the Animal's Ears; which he was to apply close for a certain Space, and by a fugitive Faculty, peculiar to the Ears of that Animal, receive immediate Benefit, either by Eructation, or Expiration, or Evomition" (p. 108). In other words, the affected person finds a cure by relieving himself of his wind. Looked at this way, if we take eructation as analogous to flatulency, the confessional booth is vaguely associated with a public privy "for the Publick Good and Ease of all such as are Hypochrondriacal, or troubled with the Cholick." Whether this association is plausible is not so important as the fact that confession is portrayed by a degrading image in a satire that "Celebrates the Church of *England* as the most perfect of all others in Discipline and Doctrine . . ." (p. 5), by ridiculing a chief antagonist, the Roman Church.

Still another invention of Peter that Swift scorns is the Papal Bulls. Punning on the word "bulls," Swift describes how Peter's bullocks or bulls crave gold so voraciously that "if *Peter* sent them abroad, though it were only upon a Compliment, they would *Roar,* and *Spit,* and *Belch,* and *Piss,* and *Fart,* and *Snivel* out *Fire,* and keep a perpetual Coyl, till you flung them a Bit of *Gold* . . ." (p. 112). These specific tantrums are "the Fulminations of the Pope threatning Hell and Damnation to those Princes who offend him" (p. 111 n.). These are all variations of a venting image, including the scatological voidings, viewed as comic.

A much more scatological and fundamental satire than these comic treatments of religious abuses is that directed against the "Learned Aeolists." Here again Swift is not satirizing Christianity or religion, as has sometimes been charged, but corruptions in religion, in particular religious enthusiasm. Swift identifies this target clearly in a note defining Aeolists as "All Pretenders to Inspiration whatsoever" (p. 150 n.), i.e., religious enthusiasts. (One of the meanings of "enthusiasm" in *NED* is "fancied inspiration.")

From the outset, Swift stresses the atheistic character of the Aeolists.

They "maintain the Original Cause of all things to be *Wind,* from which Principle this whole Universe was at first produced" (p. 150), and "Their Gods were the four *Winds,* whom they worshipped, as the Spirits that pervade and enliven the Universe, and as those from whom alone all *Inspiration* can properly be said to proceed" (p. 154). It follows that to be inspired means to be full of wind. The possibility of punning is great here. One of the meanings of the word "inspire" in *NED* is "to blow or breathe (air, etc.) upon or into."

Swift sets out to debase this notion through scatological associations. He identifies wind (Aeolists' god and religion) with flatulence. The description of one of the methods of acquiring this wind makes clear its flatulent character. Swift alleges that one may see, for instance, several hundreds of Aeolists "link'd together in a circular Chain, with every Man a Pair of Bellows applied to his Neighbour's Breech, by which they blew up each other to the Shape and Size of a *Tun.* . . . When . . . they were grown sufficiently replete, they would immediately depart, and disembogue for the Publick Good, a plentiful Share of their Acquirements into their Disciples Chaps" (p. 153). The manner of disemboguing this divine wind for the public good is equally obscene and comic, as seen in the caricature of the inspired Aeolists:

> But the great Characteristick, by which their chief Sages were best distinguished, was a certain Position of Countenance, which gave undoubted Intelligence to what Degree or Proportion, the Spirit agitated the inward Mass. For, after certain Gripings, the *Wind* and Vapours issuing forth; having first by their Turbulence and Convulsions within, caused an Earthquake in Man's little World; distorted the Mouth, bloated the Cheeks, and gave the Eyes a terrible kind of *Relievo.* At which Junctures, all their *Belches* were received for Sacred, the Sourer the better, and swallowed with infinite Consolation by their meager Devotees. And to render these yet more compleat, because the Breath of Man's Life is in his Nostrils, therefore, the choicest, most edifying, and most enlivening *Belches,* were very wisely conveyed thro' that Vehicle, to give them a Tincture as they passed.
>
> (pp. 153-54)

Swift uses scatology to suggest that the Aeolists' inspiration is a contemptuous and ludicrous delusion with no more real divinity or religion in it than empty air. Far from advocating atheism, Swift is attacking the irreligious character of enthusiasts by playing on the godlessness of their alleged inspiration.

On this basic inquiry into the character of religious enthusiasm Swift extends his satire on the various groups of dissenters. His main target is the Puritans (Aeolism is founded by Jack, the Puritan brother), as alluded to in the lampoon of the preaching scene. Dissenters are also derided in "an exact Description of the Changes made in the Face by Enthusiastick Preachers" (p. 156 n.). A note in the 1720 edition explains that "Many Dissenters, affecting extraordinary plainness and simplicity, have their Pulpits of a figure not unlike a barrel or tub" (p. 156 n.) The author describes how the priest full of wind enters this barrel, where

> a secret Funnel is also convey'd from his Posteriors, to the Bottom of the Barrel, which admits new Supplies of Inspiration from a *Northern* Chink or Crany. Whereupon, you behold him swell immediately to the Shape and Size of his *Vessel*. In this Posture he disembogues whole Tempests upon his Auditory, as the Spirit from beneath gives him Utterance; which issuing *ex adytis,* and *penetralibus,* is not performed without much Pain and Gripings. And the *Wind* in breaking forth, deals with his Face, as it does with that of the Sea; first *blackning,* then *wrinkling,* and at last *bursting it into a Foam.* It is in this Guise, the Sacred *Aeolist* delivers his oracular *Belches* to his panting Disciples; Of whom, some are greedily gaping after the sanctified Breath; others are all the while hymning out the Praises of the *Winds;* and gently wafted to and fro by their own Humming, do thus represent the soft Breezes of their Deities appeased.[33]

This is an obscene and comic picture drawn in images of flatulence uniting the priest and his audience. The priest is pictured as a puffed-up bladder belching out flatulent wind. The priest is anything but "sacred," and the process of his preaching is quite mechanistic. The audience appears hypnotized by the descending wind, which they greedily receive. The image of breaking wind is appropriate to the communion of the Aeolists and is suggestive of impure wind, as well as vices of the devilish tongue.[34]

We can easily see why this satire on religious enthusiasm may be misunderstood by those who condemn the use of scatology for any purpose, especially those who refuse to recognize scatology as a literary device. To such people the Aeolist section would be profane by the mere fact that it uses scatology, which they would presumably equate with obscenity regardless of the literary purposes it may serve. After all, they would argue, Swift did not have to use it; he could have used non-scatological language if he had wished. This argument is perfectly reasonable as far as it goes. On the other hand, if these same people read the satire with an awareness of the literary tradition of scatology, especially in satire, they would not condemn Swift outright. They would make an effort to see the possible satiric functions scatology might serve. Furthermore, if they read widely, they would be aware of certain well-known literary conventions used in satirizing the religious enthusiasts.

The work relevant to our discussion of Swift's uses of scatology in his religious satire is Henry More's *Enthusiasmus Triumphatus* (1662), a work well known to Swift's contemporaries. Swift's note in the fifth edition of the *Tale* (p. 127) testifies to his familiarity with More's work. While we cannot determine the extent of Swift's indebtedness to More, we can point out (and this is more important to our purpose) the parallel ideas in More and Swift to show that there was literary precedent for voicing certain objections to religious enthusiasm. Even a brief review of More's ideas will show that Swift was not indulging in obscenity for its own sake or originating certain ideas to discredit religion or the Church.

Nearly fifty years before the publication of the *Tale* (*Enthusiasmus* was first published in 1656), More pointed out "The great Affinity and Correspondency betwixt *Enthusiasm* and *Atheism,*" which, as we saw, Swift stresses in the Aeolist section. More's reason for connecting the enthusiasts with atheists is similar to Swift's; both see the enthusiasts as self-directed, relying on their own false inspiration, rather than seeking divine guidance. Swift ridicules this false inspiration as odious nonsense; More calls it fancy: "And the *Enthusiast*'s boldly dictating the careless ravings of his own tumultuous *Phansy* for undeniable Principles of Divine knowledge, confirms the *Atheist* that the whole business of Religion and Notion of a God is nothing but a troublesome fit of over-curious *Melancholy*" (p. 2, 1662 ed.). More and Swift both view religious enthusiasm as a delusion. More defines *enthusiasm* as "nothing else but a misconceit of being *inspired.*" He goes on to say that "Now to be *inspired* is, *to be moved in an extraordinary manner by the power or Spirit of God to act, speak, or think what is holy, just and true*. From hence it will be easily understood what *Enthusiasm* is, viz. *A full, but false, perswasion in a man that he is inspired*" (p. 2, 1662 ed.).

However, the most remarkable idea in More's work—spirit envisioned as flatulency—anticipates Swift's central metaphor in the Aeolist section:

> The *Spirit* then that wings the *Enthusiast* in such a wonderful manner, is nothing else but that *Flatulency* which is in the *Melancholy* complexion, and rises out of the *Hypochondriacal* humour upon some occasional heat, as *Winde* out of an *Aeolipila* applied to the fire. Which fume mounting into the Head, being first actuated and spirited and somewhat refined by the warmth of the Heart, fills the Mind with variety of *Imaginations*, and so quickens and inlarges *Invention*, that it makes the *Enthusiast* to admiration *fluent* and *eloquent*, he being as it were drunk with new wine drawn from that Cellar of his own that lies in the lowest region of the Body, though he be not aware of it, but takes it to be pure *Nectar*, and those waters of life that spring from above.[35]

By citing these parallel ideas in More's work, we can readily see that the scatological elements in the Aeolist section are not so much the products of Swift's imagination as they are a bold and a full treatment of conventional notions and metaphor employed earlier in discussing religious enthusiasm. Swift's possible use of current ideas does not diminish his achievement. On the contrary, the more we discover Swift's use of conventional ideas and metaphors for his own scatological satires, the more firmly we can argue for an unbiased examination of his works. Such a discovery enables us to see Swift not as a literary eccentric with "an excremental vision," but as a traditional author making imaginative and effective use of conventional materials to suit his purposes. There is an enormous difference between the relatively bare ideas and metaphors in the source work, as in More's tract, and the fully developed conceits based on these ideas and metaphors, as in the Aeolist section. As for the common charge of Swift's coarseness, we will do well to recall such scatological satire as Oldham's *Character of a certain Ugly P--* and note how much more universal and impersonal Swift's religious satire is.

Swift's moral satire includes three notorious poems: "The Lady's Dressing Room" (1730), "Cassinus and Peter" (1731), and "Strephon and Chloe" (1731),[36] commonly regarded as some of the most offensive of his scatological writings. Anyone can readily see why these poems have brought against Swift indignant protests and charges of filthy-mindedness; we would be absurd to deny his occasional excesses in describing various details connected with the heroines' private lives. I believe, however, that despite these revolting scatological elements, Swift's basic purpose in these poems is ultimately moral. I say "ultimately" because these poems are, like many other satires we have seen, medleys of a sort, composed of various elements. The most conspicuous of these elements (because most offensive) is the scatological. The climax in each of these poems is the heroes' discovery of their nymphs' humanity through the fact that these young ladies, like the heroes themselves, are subject to the necessity of evacuating. This discovery constitutes a moment of truth for these young men, to be shocked and disillusioned, and in the case of "Strephon and Chloe," to become cynical. The scatological elements in these poems, however, do not suggest, as John Middleton Murry asserts, Swift's loathing of "woman as a physical being" or his horror at the fact of her "physical evacuation."[37] On the contrary, the scatological elements dramatize the failure of people, as represented by the young heroes, to reconcile the physical imperfections and animal nature of man with his decent and spiritual side. To say it another way, the poems through the scatological elements broadly suggest the potentially tragic consequence of one's inability to come to terms with reality.

The immediate consequence of the hero's failure to accept his nymph's humanity in the Celia poems ("The Lady's Dressing Room" and "Cassinus and Peter") is, on the whole, comic; even so, we may easily see its potential tragedy. The young hero of "The Lady's Dressing Room" becomes obsessed with the fact that his nymph has physical necessities like his own. Before his discovery of this fact, he had suffered a romantic delusion concerning Celia and other nymphs like her; after his discovery and consequent disillusionment, he turns to the other extreme so that

> His foul Imagination links
> Each Dame he sees with all her Stinks:
> And, if unsav'ry Odours fly,
> Conceives a Lady standing by.
>
> (ll. 121-24)

The experience of another starry-eyed young hero of "Cassinus and Peter" is no less traumatic. As the immediate result of his discovery, he loses his wits and is, for the time being at least, utterly heartbroken. On the other hand, the same kind of discovery in "Strephon and Chloe" makes the hero cynical and vulgar. In a way he too loses his wits, but instead of becoming brokenhearted, the more aggressive Strephon turns into a vulgarian and deliberately taunts his bride with "a Rouzer in her Face" (l. 192). The tragedy or potential tragedy of one's failure to reconcile reality with decency is all too clear. In the case of the married couple, life loses all civility and grace. For the young men of the Celia poems, their life—for the time being, if not forever—offers no possibility of beauty or joy or love, but only signs of vile human imperfection everywhere.

An equally conspicuous element in these poems is the element of humor. We recall the humorous images of the swain suffering from "amorous Fits" in "The Lady's Dressing Room" and the young scholar suffering from despondency in "Cassinus and Peter"; we also remember the groom in "Strephon and Chloe," whose "Night-Cap border'd round with Lace/ Could give no Softness to his Face" (ll. 93-94), loathing "His prickled Beard, and hairy Breast" (l. 92), struggling to approach his "Nymph" and "Goddess," who turns out to be to his consternation and indignation, a mere mortal like himself. More fundamentally comic is the parody of classical similes and stock figures of romantic heroines. Herbert Davis points out that "'The Lady's Dressing Room' is full of parodies of all the overused classical tags and stories in English poetry from Milton to Pope."[38] Strephon's opening of Celia's chest, which leads to his awful discovery, is expressively humorous because of the following parody of the story of Pandora's box. A whole line is borrowed from *Paradise Lost* at the end:[39]

He lifts the Lid, there needs no more,
He smelt it all the Time before.
As from within *Pandora*'s Box,
When *Epimetheus* op'd the Locks,
A sudden universal Crew
Of humane Evils upwards flew;
He still was comforted to find
That *Hope* at last remain'd behind;
So *Strephon* lifting up the Lid,
To view what in the Chest was hid.
The Vapours flew from out the Vent,
But *Strephon* cautious never meant
The Bottom of the Pan to grope,
And fowl his Hands in Search of *Hope*.
O never may such vile Machine
Be once in *Celia*'s Chamber seen!
O may she better learn to keep
"Those Secrets of the hoary deep!

(ll. 81-98)

Swift immediately provides another parody in an extended simile (ll. 99-114) "built up," as Davis notes, "so elaborately out of a detailed and vivid description of a piece of meat roasting on the spit, which has been carefully prepared as the laws of cookery require, but which is ruined if the fat drops on a cinder—'To stinking Smoak it turns the Flame/ Pois'ning the Flesh from whence it came' " (ll. 105-06).[40] The parody here is also a humorous exaggeration of Strephon's discovery; it is an ironic comment on his total collapse when he learns the truth about his nymph. The irony lies in the fact that Celia's image need not be ruined by his discovery of the truth, which is not a personal blemish peculiar to one maid, but a universal fact applicable to all maidens and all men. By magnifying Celia's one human imperfection out of proportion, Strephon distorts her image so drastically that he figuratively ruins her and all other maidens as well.

In "Cassinus and Peter," subtitled "A Tragical Elegy," the humor of the parody on well-known classical stories is heightened, because here Swift renders the parody through the mouth of Cassinus "swallow'd up in Spleen" (l. 10), whose brain is, as Swift would say, "overheated" with his awful secret. Cassinus thinks he is dying, mortally wounded by "*Caelia*'s horrid Fact" (l. 93), and sees "a vision of Virgil's hell,"[41] described in part by a line from Shakespeare's *Macbeth:*

> And there—behold *Alecto* stand,
> A Whip of Scorpions in her Hand.
> Lo, *Charon* from his leaky Wherry,
> Beck'ning to waft me o'er the Ferry.
> I come, I come,—*Medusa,* see,
> Her Serpents hiss direct at me.
> Begone; unhand me, hellish Fry;
> Avaunt—ye cannot say 'twas I.[42]

Persuaded by Peter to divulge the secret, Cassinus prepares Peter for the "horrid Fact" in words that parody Ovid's story of the secret of Midas whispering to the reeds:[43]

Now, bend thine Ear; since out it must:
But, when thou seest me laid in Dust,
The Secret thou shalt ne'er impart;
Not to the Nymph that keeps thy Heart;
(How would her Virgin Soul bemoan
A Crime to all her Sex unknown!)
Nor whisper to the tattling Reeds,
The blackest of all Female Deeds.[44]

Swift indulges in parody at the expense of the young man. The humor lies in the discrepancy between the kind of secret with which Cassinus struggles and the manner of his struggle which is indicated in his language full of classical allusions. The effect is ironical, anticlimactic, and comic.

An element of parody in "Strephon and Chloe" also deals with one characteristic that runs through all three poems, namely an unrealistic, foolish, and childish point of view toward women and life. The "horrid Fact" hits the young men hard because they identified their nymphs with the nymphs of the storybooks in which unreal beings lead unreal lives marked by no unpleasant facts. Whatever one may call such a point of view, unrealistic or romantic, it comes under corrective treatment in Swift's satire. Swift, of course, did not assign pastoral names without good reason; he specifically refers to heroic swains and ever-fresh nymphs. We may recall Cassinus' pleas to his imagined audience:

Yet, kind *Arcadians,* on my Urn
These Elegies and Sonnets burn,
And on the Marble grave these Rhimes,
A Monument to after-Times:
"Here *Cassy* lies, by *Caelia* slain,
"And dying, never told his Pain.
(ll. 73-78)

Swift smiles at this kind of comic nonsense in an obviously ironic tone in "Strephon and Chloe," whose opening lines we may cite here.

Of *Chloe* all the Town has rung;
By ev'ry size of Poets sung:
So beautiful a Nymph appears
But once in Twenty Thousand Years.
But Nature form'd with nicest Care,
And, faultless to a Single Hair.
Her graceful Mein, her Shape, and Face,
Confest her of no mortal Race:
And then, so nice, and so genteel;
Such Cleanliness from Head to Heel:
No Humours gross, or frowzy Steams,
No noisom Whiffs, or sweaty Streams,
Before, behind, above, below,
Could from her taintless Body flow.
Would so discreetly Things dispose,
None ever saw her pluck a Rose.
Her dearest Comrades never caught her
Squat on her Hams, to make Maid's Water.
You'd swear, that so divine a Creature
Felt no Necessities of Nature.

(ll. 1-20)

Maurice Johnson, quoting lines 15-18 above, comments: "That is surprising and witty parody of the nymphs of poetry whose only necessity in life is to charm sighs from an inexhaustible retinue of shepherds whose only necessity, in turn, is to be charmed, and whose sheep, if there were enough to go around, must certainly have wandered from the enameled plains and perished" (p. 95). The young men are all victims of their own confusion—they confound fiction with reality, failing to enjoy fiction as fiction.

Interwoven with the scatological and humorous elements in these poems is the moral element. We have already noted how the scatological and humorous elements contribute to Swift's moral purposes, such as discrediting a false notion concerning maidens and exposing the ludicrous consequences of adhering to such a notion. It remains for us to consider other moral implications of the poems. Though we have noted Swift's censure of the young heroes of the poems, there is also considerable satire toward the heroines as well. In "The Lady's Dressing Room," Swift exposes Celia as a creature of cunning and filth. She is seen as a perfect example of the discrepancy we often find between appearance and reality. This discrepancy is all the more shocking because her appearance is so fair and her private habits so foul. The merciless catalog of Celia's personal and cosmetic items is used to shatter man's romantic nonsense about the fairest of ladies whom he usually creates in his own imagination; it is also used for the benefit of those ladies who may be guilty of such defects as uncleanliness and deception.[45] Celia's deception is evident in the array of cosmetic aids she employs to hide her physical blemishes, not so much out of her feminine modesty to avoid offending others as out of her overriding desire to dazzle innocent swains with her painted face.[46] Closely linked to her deception is her uncleanliness, which comes in for Swift's severe censure.

In "Strephon and Chloe" the object of Swift's stricture is not such incurable imperfections as physical blemishes, but moral and intellectual blemishes, which may be diminished or even removed. Chloe is depicted as a beautiful maid with a shallow mind and little sense of such feminine virtues as modesty or decency. In the opening lines of the poem, we see a picture of Chloe in the ethereal image of popular storybook heroines; then we are rudely jolted by Strephon's discovery of her humanity and his vulgarity on the nuptial bed. While Strephon is portrayed as guilty of starting their marriage in a vulgar manner and thereby setting the tone to their marriage, Swift makes it clear that Chloe shares the blame for the kind of life they lead. For, the second picture of Chloe emerges in the poem as a woman equally vulgar and coarse, with no sense of taste, a contemptible creature indeed. "They soon from all Constraint are freed" (l. 205), Swift observes, and they look at life about them through eyes which admit no beauty: "And, by the beastly way of Thinking,/ Find great Society in Stinking" (ll. 209-10). If the first picture of Chloe is unreal, the second picture is real in a most unattractive way. Having drawn these two pictures as extreme examples of womanhood, Swift comments on certain defects characteristic of all such women. In particular he condemns vices of the tongue, ladies' affectation "To pass for Wits before a Rake" (l. 268), their malicious backbiting, and "rank Imagination" (l. 279). His admonition against ladies' intellectual blemishes gains added force because at first Chloe is thought to have no human body and later is found to be primarily body. It is against this general disparagement of harebrained ladies that Swift closes the poem with an earnest counsel to all women and men:

> On Sense and Wit your Passion found,
> By Decency cemented round;
> Let Prudence with Good Nature strive,
> To keep Esteem and Love alive.
> Then come old Age whene'er it will,
> Your Friendship shall continue still:
> And thus a mutual gentle Fire,
> Shall never but with Life expire.[47]

We may pause here briefly to say that we should not make the mistake of accusing Swift of misogyny or of loathing "woman as a physical being." His stricture against Celia's uncleanliness suggests his hatred of feminine dissimulation and vanity, but not hatred of women. This distinction is important. If we may go outside the poems here, we may recall his *Letter to a Young Lady, on her Marriage* (1723). Though the letter was written some eight years before the poems (1730-31), Swift's advice to the young woman on cleanliness brings to mind his censure concerning Celia's squalid habits. He assures the young lady that men will pay for their wives' clothes

> if the Ladies will but allow a suitable Addition of Care in the Cleanliness and Sweetness of their Persons: For, the satyrical Part of Mankind will needs believe, that it is not impossible, to be very fine and very filthy; and that the Capacities of a Lady are sometimes apt to fall short in cultivating Cleanliness and Finery

> together. I shall only add, upon so tender a Subject, what a pleasant Gentleman said concerning a silly Woman of Quality; that nothing could make her supportable but cutting off her Head; for his Ears were offended by her Tongue, and his Nose by her Hair and Teeth.[48]

We may also observe that nowhere in the three poems does Swift condemn female fashion. His comments in the *Letter* clearly indicate that he is against extravagant fashion, but not unobtrusive fashion.[49]

We may further consider larger moral implications of the three poems as a whole. In these poems Swift advocates a balanced view of human nature based on human facts. On one hand, as in the Celia poems, Swift disparages the romantic view of humanity, which cannot stand the test of day-to-day living; on the other hand, he equally disparages, as in "Strephon and Chloe," the view of humanity based on physical nature alone, which ignores intellectual and moral virtues. Closely related to this idea is a plea for clarity of vision when we look at life about us. Like Bacon, Swift clearly recognizes that human beings tend to delude themselves and see order and beauty where none exists. Swift seems to imply in these poems that life based on delusion usually ends in bitter disappointment or even tragedy.[50] He also comments on the relationship between the sexes, particularly among the married. He does not deny the place of physical love ("passion") in marriage, but neither does he approve of a life of unrestrained passion. Swift would agree that marriage without passion is unrealistic; he would also agree that marriage based on passion alone is just as undesirable. Neither is a reasonable situation, he would say. What he suggests is a marriage of the two—the body and the mind—in some measure of harmony and balance, an ideal applicable to all human life and conduct.

We can now see that Swift in these notorious poems employs scatology as an important device to achieve moral didacticism. It is used for shock value as in the Celia poems where the romantic swains lose their wits; at the same time, it is used to produce disgust and nausea in us. We are appalled, as the young lover was so distressed, at the shocking discrepancy between Celia's fair exterior and her foul necessities. We are also offended at Strephon's conduct on his marriage bed and at Chloe's subsequent vulgarity. If Swift's use of scatology at times seems to be excessive, as in the catalog of Celia's belongings, his basic purpose is to emphasize his point, to provoke maximum shock, disgust, nausea, or disillusionment. Thus, just as Swift in these poems employs humor in the form of parody mainly to ridicule and deride overly romantic swains, and not for pointless laughter, so he employs scatology mainly to make us disgusted with the nymphs, and not for pointless sensationalism.

In reply to popular criticism, Swift himself wrote a humorous apologia for the Celia poems under the title *A Modest Defence of a Late Poem (By an Unkown Author, call'd, The LADY'S Dressing-ROOM)* (1732).[51] In a humorous tone, but not entirely devoid of some seriousness (his humor is rarely pointless), Swift notes that the poem has "so highly inflamed the whole Sex, (except a very few of better Judgment)" and confesses that he "cannot but lament the prevailing ill Taste among us which is not able to discover that useful Satyr running through every Line, and the Matter as decently wrapp'd up, as it is possible the Subject could bear." He then delivers a satiric sting directed at his critics by way of explaining a moral theme in the poem.

> *Cleanliness* hath, in all polite Ages and Nations, been esteemed the chief corporeal Perfection in *Women,* as it is well known to those who are conversant with the antient *Poets.* And so it is still among the young People of Judgment and Sobriety, when they are disposed to marry. And I do not doubt, but that there is a great Number of young Ladies in this Town and Kingdom, who in reading that Poem, find great Complacency in their own Minds, from a Consciousness that the Satyrical Part in the *Lady's Dressing Room,* does not in the least affect them.

"Wherefore it is manifest," Swift declares, "that no *Poem* was ever written with a better Design for the Service of the *Sex* . . ." (p. 338).[52]

Intellectual Satire

We have observed that intellectual satire is a favorite conventional topic of scatological writings among English authors. In reading Swift's scatological writings, it is important to remember the literary tradition of intellectual satire, for without a knowledge of this background, the psychoanalytical or biographically-oriented reader may mistake the scatological elements in Swift's intellectual satire as further evidence of the author's excremental vision. We may begin a survey of the principal scatological passages in Swift's intellectual satire by examining Norman Brown's psychoanalytical treatment of a scatological reference.

"Strephon and Chloe"[53] contains the following passage about "What various Ways our Females take,/ To pass for Wits before a Rake!" (ll. 267-68):

> But, sure a Tell-tale out of School
> Is of all Wits the greatest Fool;
> Whose rank Imagination fills,
> Her Heart, and from her Lips distills;
> You'd think she utter'd from behind,
> Or at her Mouth was breaking Wind.
> (ll. 277-82)

Brown cites the last couplet (ll. 281-82) as evidence of "Swift's vision of sublimated anality" in his writings.[54] We need not be expert psychoanalysts to question this interpretation on the ground of literary facts, for we can see that Brown ignores the conventional figure that suggests that breaking wind is equivalent to tattling. Perhaps I misread Brown completely, but the impression I receive is that Brown thinks Swift rather unique in using this figure of speech. We have seen that this is not the case. *The Benefit of Farting* (1722), for example, makes fun of the close relationship between flatulency and women's talkativeness.[55]

Brown further declares, "And more generally, as Greenacre observes, there is throughout Swift 'a kind of linking of the written or printed word with the excretory functions.'"[56] He reminds us of

Swift's "references to literary polemics (his own literary form) as dirt-throwing (compare the Yahoos)" (p. 198). Again, this evidence is questionable on the ground of literary facts, for "references to literary polemics . . . as dirt-throwing" are quite commonplace (for example, Pope's reference in *The Dunciad* to the diving contest of the party-writers).[57]

Brown also cites a passage from *A Letter of Advice to a Young Poet* (1721) as another evidence of "a kind of linking of the written or printed word with the excretory functions." Swift refers to bad writing as excremental and playfully suggests that since the town has so many bad writers who threaten to infect everyone with their excremental writings, these authors should be confined in a Grub Street to prevent the town from becoming a common jakes. The following is the passage Brown cites:

> When writers of all sizes, like freemen of cities, are at liberty to throw out their filth and excrementitious productions, in every street as they please, what can the consequence be, but the town must be poisoned and become such another jakes, as by report of great travellers, Edinburgh is at night.[58]

"This train of thought," Brown observes, "is so characteristically Swift's . . ." (p. 199). It is, in the sense that in his scorn of inferior authors Swift commonly refers to bad writing as excrement. In *The Battle of the Books,* Swift describes the spider, the emblem of modern writers he scorns, as "That which by a lazy Contemplation of four Inches round; by an over-weening Pride, which feeding and engendering on it self, turns all into Excrement and Venom . . ." (p. 232). Elsewhere in the satire, he argues that "if the materials be nothing but Dirt, spun out of your own Entrails (the Guts of *Modern* Brains) the Edifice will conclude at last in a *Cobweb* . . ." (p. 234).[59]

Brown neglects to add, however, that "this train of thought . . . so characteristically Swift's" is a reflection of a common figure of speech used for bad writing that goes back to Catallus' "cacata charta." Among Swift's English predecessors we have seen in Nashe's *Pierce Penilesse* (1592) the hero's warning against inferior writings reminiscent of the passage from Swift's *Letter of Advice* quoted above: "Looke to it, you Booksellers and Stationers, and let not your shops be infected with any such goose gyblets or stinking garbadge, as the Iygs of newsmongers, and especiallie such of you as frequent Westminster hall, let them be circumspect what dunghill papers they bring hither: for one pamphlet is enough to raise a damp that may poison a whole Tearme. . . ."[60]

Swift, of course, does not limit scatological satire to vices of language. He also employs scatology in attacking vices and abuses of mind, man's most prized possession. In *A Tale of a Tub,* Swift attacks certain literary critics for their malicious criticism, which he sees as an abuse of mind and of learning. Swift does not say that all critics are equally bad or abominable. He classifies critics into three sorts. The first is the judicious, fair-minded critic who helps the reader appreciate the work, its defects as well as its merits. The second is the textual critic, "the Restorers of Antient Learning from the Worms." Swift sees these two kinds of critics as acceptable, and he remarks that they "have been for some Ages utterly extinct." He views the third kind of critic differently. Maintaining this ironic tone, Swift declares that "The Third, and Noblest Sort, is that of the TRUE CRITICK, whose Original is the most Antient of all" (p. 93). "The proper Employment of a *True Antient Genuine Critick* . . ." Swift asserts, "is, to travel thro' this vast World of Writings: to pursue and hunt those Monstrous Faults bred within them: to drag out the lurking Errors like *Cacus* from his Den; to multiply them like *Hydra*'s Heads; and rake them together like *Augeas*'s Dung." Swift goes on to define that "a *True Critic* . . . is *a Discoverer and Collector of Writers Faults*" (p. 95). The scatological passage appears, however, not in a description of the true critic, but in a description of the first kind, the judicious critic. These judicious critics, Swift explains, "In their common perusal of Books" single out

> the Errors and Defects, the Nauseous, the Fulsome, the Dull, and the Impertinent, with the Caution of a Man that walks thro' *Edenborough* Streets in a Morning, who is indeed as careful as he can, to watch diligently, and spy out the Filth in his Way, not that he

> is curious to observe the Colour and Complexion of the Ordure, or take its Dimensions, much less to be padling in, or tasting it: but only with a Design to come out as cleanly as he may.
>
> (pp. 92-93)

The passage is marked by scatological humor heightened by an insinuating tone and is applicable to the true critic, the "Discoverer and Collector of Writers Faults." The true critic (the third group) and the judicious critic (the first group) are diametrically opposed in their handling of writers' faults. One revels in them, the other does not; one "rake[s] them together like *Augeas*'s Dung," the other treats them "with the Caution of a Man that walks thro' *Edenborough* Streets . . . to come out as cleanly as he may." If I am guilty of twisting Swift's text to suit my purpose, I may at least suspect here (to borrow Swift's phrase) "a very seasonable *Innuendo*" on the true critic, especially since much of the digression on critics, as elsewhere in the *Tale,* is characterized by a kind of crazy hedging and cross reference.

Far more devastating intellectual satire is contained in the famous ninth section of the *Tale,* where Swift uproots the source of human pride, man's achievements in politics, religion, and philosophy. This is perhaps the strongest attack on man, who fancies himself the most superior being on the earth by virtue of his reason. Swift does not downgrade reason, but shows how easily it becomes a slave to blind human passions. He would have the proud man see how he has used (or not used) his reason. This he does by a frontal assault on a grand scale with a shattering proposition that madness, i.e., the failure of reason, is the foundation of man's proud achievements in history. And madness, Swift declares, is caused not by excess of divine inspiration or any such glorious idea, but by vapors, those arising from man's "lower Faculties," i.e., the genital and excretory organs. The imagery he employs in explaining the theory of vapors and their effect on the brain is scatological as a means of stressing the low nature of these vapors:

> the *upper Region* of Man, is furnished like the *middle Region* of the Air; The Materials are formed from Causes of the widest Difference, yet produce at last the same Substance and Effect.

> Mists arise from the Earth, Steams from Dunghills, Exhalations from the Sea, and Smoak from Fire; yet all Clouds are the same in Composition, as well as Consequences: and the Fumes issuing from a Jakes, will furnish as comely and useful a Vapor, as Incense from an Altar . . . then it will follow, that as the Face of Nature never produces Rain, but when it is overcast and disturbed, so Human Understanding, seated in the Brain, must be troubled and overspread by Vapours, ascending from the lower Faculties, to water the Invention, and render it fruitful.
>
> (p.163)

To make sure that the reader understands what the "lower Faculties" refer to, Swift cites two historical events set off by madness vapors. Henry IV of France readies his armed forces to the consternation of the neighboring countries because, as it turns out later, he could not ravish a certain lady, "whose Eyes had raised a Protuberancy, and before Emission, she was removed into an Enemy's Country" (p. 164). The other example concerns Louis XIV, whose military campaigns rage on until the vapors descend to form a "fistula in ano" (p. 166).

The scatological details in the digression on madness, including the tour of the excremental Bedlam, comprise only a small portion of the whole, but they give an unmistakable quality to the entire section. It is on these fundamental theories of vapor and brain that Swift rests his attack on the failure of reason, the direct attack being made in non-scatological language. This, of course, does not mean that Swift is against all politics, religion, philosophy, or literature. Swift is against what he considers to be manifestations of insanity or pride in these fields. He suggests that needless bloodshed, unorthodox sects, atheistic philosophies are all caused by failure of reason. Fundamentally it is this failure of reason that Swift attacks through scatology.

For, failure of reason engenders madness and allows this madness to possess a man. If reason had control over the senses, fancy would not build on the senses all sorts of delusions, including self-complacency and the illusion of happiness. It is when reason loses control over the senses that the excess of vapors from the lower faculties disturbs the brain, which in turn clouds human understanding and spins out insane schemes and notions. In Swift's famous words, "when a Man's Fancy gets *astride* on his Reason, when Imagination is at Cuffs with the Senses, and common Understanding, as well as common Sense, is Kickt out of Doors; the first Proselyte he makes, is Himself . . ." (p. 171). When fiction takes hold of man's imagination or vice versa, man blinds himself to moral reality about him and becomes impervious to conditions that should provoke fierce indignation in a man of reason. Worse yet, such a man becomes a victim of presumption about his own moral and intellectual perfection.

The attack on the failure of reason is, of course, an attack on pride itself. Scatology is particularly appropriate in such an attack, because it forces man to see his real self including his body, which in certain respects does not differ very much from that of other animals. Such a body should remind man of the imperfect and limited nature of his being, and such recognition should instill in him a measure of humility about himself.

It now remains for us to examine Swift's uses of scatology in *Gulliver's Travels*.

4

Scatology in *Gulliver's Travels*

Although scatology appears in only a small part of *Gulliver's Travels* (1726), it is obviously an important satirical device.[1] If we exclude the scatological passages and references or read an edition that bowdlerizes them, we see immediately that the book would lose much of its disconcerting tonal effect. Swift does not achieve this effect by resorting to scatology indiscriminately. He employs the device as particular situations and purposes demand it, to reinforce non-scatological satire, amuse with scatological humor, or disgust with loathsome details. His use of scatology is also marked by modulation of tone and emphasis; it can be matter-of-fact, humorous, or crudely satirical. Furthermore, Swift rarely abuses or wastes scatology for sensationalism alone; few scatological passages are irrelevant to his satiric purposes.

Gulliver's Travels characteristically intermingles the humorous and the satiric. The passages of scatological humor number only a few, but they serve Swift's various purposes. In Book I, we find three scatological passages, all primarily humorous. The first two capitalize on acts of natural necessity, and the third concerns Gulliver's adventure in extinguishing the fire at the palace. Swift mentions one of these acts in the opening chapter of Book I. Although Gulliver is a prisoner and is tied down on a cart surrounded by swarms of tiny but well-armed Lilliputians, he is forced to relieve himself. He recalls his experience:

> Soon after I heard a general Shout . . . and I felt great Numbers of the People on my Left Side relaxing the Cords to such a Degree, that I was able to turn upon my Right, and to ease my self with making Water; which I very plentifully did, to the great Astonishment of the People, who conjecturing by my Motions what I was going to do, immediately opened to the right and left on that Side, to avoid the Torrent which fell with such Noise and Violence from me.
>
> (I.i.25)

This account is factual, but a couple of pages later in the beginning of the second chapter, where we see Gulliver chained to his temple-house, we read a detailed account of the way he met "the Necessities of Nature" in his distressing circumstance. The defensive tone and euphemism add to the humor of the passage:

> I had been for some Hours extremely pressed by the Necessities of Nature; which was no Wonder, it being almost two Days since I had last disburthened myself. I was under great Difficulties between Urgency and Shame. The best Expedient I could think on, was to creep into my House, which I accordingly did; and shutting the Gate after me, I went as far as the Length of my Chain would suffer; and discharged my Body of that uneasy Load. But this was the only Time I was ever guilty of so uncleanly an Action; for which I cannot but hope the candid Reader will give some Allowance, after he hath maturely and impartially considered my Case, and the Distress I was in.
>
> (I.ii.29)

Here Swift is obviously indulging in scatological humor, for Gulliver goes on to relate how he solved this vexing problem and apologizes further for mentioning the incident:

> From this Time my constant Practice was, as soon as I rose, to perform that Business in open Air, at the full Extent of my Chain; and due Care was taken every Morning before Company came, that the offensive Matter should be carried off in Wheel-

> barrows, by two Servants appointed for that Purpose. I would not have dwelt so long upon a Circumstance, that perhaps at first Sight may appear not very momentous; if I had not thought it necessary to justify my Character in Point of Cleanliness to the World; which I am told, some of my Maligners have been pleased, upon this and other Occasions, to call in Question.
>
> (I.ii.29)

The humor increases when we consider the logic of Gulliver's apology and his subsequent action. While Gulliver "thought it necessary to justify" his "Character in Point of Cleanliness to the World," he seeks to establish his cleanliness by telling his audience at some length about his method of relieving himself and removing "the offensive Matter."[2]

Though Gulliver insists that "this was the only Time I was ever guilty of so uncleanly an Action," he later commits an offensive act in putting out the fire at the Lilliputian palace. Summoned to help put out the fire, Gulliver rushes to the scene, only to discover that the fire is too strong to be put out by water thrown out of buckets "about the Size of a large Thimble." Under the desperate circumstance, Gulliver is again forced to resort to "an Expedient" which, in the eyes of the queen, proves to be an unpardonable act of indecency. Gulliver relates that momentous adventure with a tinge of excitement and satisfaction:

> I might easily have stifled it [the fire] with my Coat, which I unfortunately left behind me for haste, and came away only in my Leathern Jerkin. The Case seemed wholly desperate and deplorable; and this magnificent Palace would have infallibly been burnt down to the Ground, if, by a Presence of Mind, unusual to me, I had not suddenly thought of an Expedient. I had the Evening before drank plentifully of a most delicious Wine, called *Glimigrim* . . . which is very diuretick. By the luckiest Chance in the World, I had not discharged myself of any Part of it. The Heat I had contracted by coming very near the Flames, and by my labouring to quench them, made the Wine begin to operate by Urine; which I voided in such a Quantity, and applied so well to the proper Places, that in three Minutes the Fire was

> wholly extinguished; and the rest of that noble Pile, which had cost so many Ages in erecting, preserved from Destruction.
> (I.v.56)

The main and immediate effect of the episode is humorous. If there is an element of satire here, it is not readily discernible. We smile at Gulliver towering over the palace in the act of rendering his service to the crown in a most extraordinary manner, for (as the saying goes) "Foul water will quench fire as well as fair," while at the same time we sympathize with the outraged queen for having to suffer such indignity. We are also aware that Gulliver's intentions are good; for this reason we sympathize with him also, especially when his powerful enemies at the court cite this incident, along with his earlier refusal to abduct the remaining fleet of Blesfuscu, as evidence of treason ("by the fundamental Laws of the Realm, it is Capital in any Person, of what Quality soever, to make water within the Precincts of the Palace" [I.v.56]). The humor lies not only in the irony of the outcome of the action, but also in the relationship of Gulliver and the queen. Even though the queen is the captor of this giant, she cannot extinguish the fire and must endure the indignity of the offensive action committed by her captive.[3]

Swift extends scatological humor at Gulliver's expense to Book II of the *Travels.* Interestingly enough, the first instance of such humor appears, as in Book I, in the opening chapter and concerns again Gulliver's relieving of himself. Gulliver, who has been placed on the huge bed of the Brobdingnagian farmer (who discovered Gulliver on his farm), finds himself constrained with "some natural Necessities":

> I was pressed to do more than one Thing, which another could not do for me; and therefore endeavoured to make my Mistress understand that I desired to be set down on the Floor; which after she had done, my Bashfulness would not suffer me to express my self farther than by pointing to the Door, and bowing several Times. The good Woman with much Difficulty at last perceived what I would be at; and taking me up again in her Hand, walked into the Garden where she set me down. I went on one Side about

> two Hundred Yards; and beckoning to her not to look or to follow me, I hid my self between two Leaves of Sorrel, and there discharged the Necessities of Nature.
>
> (II.i.93-94)

Gulliver's euphemism in the opening sentence is as charming as his bashfulness, and the care he takes to hide himself from the farmer's wife is amusing, especially since the giant woman is not likely to see very clearly such a tiny Tom Thumb-like creature. It is also amusing to note that Gulliver's assertion of self-importance is more forceful in the land of the giants than in that of the pygmies. This assertion of his dignity, coupled with his insistence upon reporting in detail "so uncleanly an Action," provokes a smile from us.

Immediately following this passage Gulliver apologizes in a mock-serious tone for mentioning such offensive particulars. The tone betrays Swift's humor:

> I hope, the gentle Reader will excuse me for dwelling on these and the like Particulars; which however insignificant they may appear to grovelling vulgar Minds, yet will certainly help a Philosopher to enlarge his Thoughts and Imagination, and apply them to the Benefit of publick as well as private Life; which was my sole Design in presenting this and other Accounts of my Travels to the World; wherein I have been chiefly studious of Truth, without affecting any Ornaments of Learning, or of Style.
>
> (II.i.94)

In its defensive tone, this apology reminds us of the earlier one offered by Gulliver concerning his act of necessity while he was chained to his temple-house in Lilliput. The humor lies in its implication. Despite Gulliver's assurance, "grovelling vulgar Minds" may wonder how this description "will certainly help a Philosopher to enlarge his Thoughts and Imagination, and apply them to the Benefit of publick as well as private Life." Unless he is a simple-minded fool, however, no "gentle Reader" will search for some hidden profundity in this passage or fail to appreciate its mock-serious humor.[4]

This and the two other similar passages cited earlier (Gulliver tied on the cart and later chained in the temple-house) are the only passages in the *Travels* that describe in some detail Gulliver's acts of necessity. Though these passages are obviously humorous and apparently non-satirical, when considered in the context of the whole book, in a roundabout way they ultimately serve the basic satiric purpose in the book. For, partly through these unpleasant facts we are not allowed to forget that Gulliver is a physical being. It is worth noting that these details appear in the first two chapters of the first voyage and the first chapter of the second voyage, as though the early reference to these unpleasant necessities establishes and stresses Gulliver's physical nature. This is an important point in the entire satire on human pride, because Swift attacks man's exalted view of himself partly by probing man's animal nature and by relating him to Yahoo.

The second scatological passage in Book II has to do with Gulliver's fall into cow dung. The episode occurs while Gulliver is taking a leisurely and solitary walk in the country free from the watchful eyes of his nurse. He recalls his unfortunate experience:

> There was a Cow-dung in the Path, and I must needs try my Activity by attempting to leap over it. I took a Run, but unfortunately jumped short, and found my self just in the Middle up to my Knees. I waded through with some Difficulty, and one of the Footmen wiped me as clean as he could with his Handkerchief; for I was filthily bemired, and my Nurse confined me to my Box until we returned home; where the Queen was soon informed of what had passed, and the Footmen spread it about the Court; so that all the Mirth, for some Days, was at my Expence. (II.v.124)

This is funny, to be sure, but we must realize that Gulliver is not wholly blameless. His vision gradually becomes accustomed to the gigantic proportions of the land, and he finally fancies himself to be much larger than he is so that when he sees his tiny image in the mirror beside the image of a giant, he imagines himself "dwindled many Degrees below" his "usual Size" (II.iii.107). After all, he decides to jump, full of playful conceit and self-confidence. This mishap serves to deflate his over-confidence in himself.

In a number of episodes preceding this unfortunate mishap, Gulliver is made aware of his vulnerable and insignificant status. He is forced to guard himself against bread crusts, hailstones, and common flies. He also suffers from the pranks of the dwarf (whom he contemptuously identifies as the shortest person in the kingdom, "not full Thirty Foot high") as well as the whim of a monkey, the "odious Animal" that to his mortification seems to take him "for a young one of his own Species" (as later to his horror the inflamed female Yahoo takes him for a Yahoo). The cow-dung episode underscores a series of these anticlimactic incidents that diminish Gulliver's notion of self-importance.

The final scatological passage in Book II concerns Gulliver's experience with the Brobdingnagian flies, "odious Insects, each of them as big as a *Dunstable* Lark":

> They would sometimes alight upon my Victuals, and leave their loathsome Excrement or Spawn behind, which to me was very visible, although not to the Natives of that Country, whose large Opticks were not so acute as mine in viewing smaller Objects. Sometimes they would fix upon my Nose or Forehead, where they stung me to the Quick, smelling very offensively; and I could easily trace that viscous Matter, which our Naturalists tell us enables those Creatures to walk with their Feet upwards upon a Cieling.
>
> (II.iii.109)

Through this magnified detail Swift points out the vile facts of human life, which escape our attention only because of our inability to notice them without the aid of a microscope. In the context of Swift's probing of certain unpleasant aspects of the human body to be found beneath a pleasing surface, this scatological passage reinforces the non-scatological but ugly passages that reveal the blemishes of skin found among the Brobdingnagian ladies and in Gulliver (II.i.91-92; v.118-19).[5] In both instances Swift challenges man's complacent view of himself and life about him through the presentation of facts that have been ignored or unexamined.

Beginning with Book III of the *Travels* scatology takes on a pointedly satirical and much more shocking turn. The kind of playful scatological humor we have seen in the first two voyages disappears. In Book III Swift uses scatology exclusively in Gulliver's report of his visit to the Academy of Lagado where the targets of scatological satire are scientific, medical, and political projectors.[6] The satire directed against these targets is delivered in some of the crudest scatology in the *Travels*. Evidently even Arbuthnot was disturbed by the satire, which he read in manuscript form. He writes to Swift: "As for your book, . . . before you put the finishing hand to it, it is really necessary to be acquainted with some new improvements of mankind, that have appeared of late, and are daily appearing."[7] When Swift published the book without softening the satire, Arbuthnot voiced his disapproval to Swift: "I tell you freely, the part of the projectors is the least brilliant."[8]

Granted that Swift's motive is beyond reproach, some of the most sympathetic readers may be at a loss to justify certain experiments Swift has Gulliver report. One of the most revolting is the "Operation to reduce human Excrement to its original Food" (III.v.180). None of us can deny that the detailed description of this experiment is most nauseating, but even here Swift is not merely dabbling in excrement for its own sake or for sensationalism. He is obviously exercising the conventional satiric license of exaggeration. More obviously, however, as numerous critics have pointed out and as we may remember from the first chapter of my discussion, the passage here recalls Rabelais' excremental description of virtuosos belonging to the Queen of Quintessence in language and imagery that suggest Swift's close knowledge, if not a close imitation, of it.[9]

Similarly, the satiric aim in the scatological description of other experiments emerges when we realize that Swift was parodying experiments proposed or conducted in England and abroad. One such example is "plowing the Ground with Hogs . . . at the same time manuring it with their Dung" (III.v.180). As Miss Nicolson and Miss

Mohler have demonstrated, this agricultural experiment suggests Swift's familiarity with the report of a similar method used in growing tobacco in Ceylon.[10] Another revolting experiment is a cure of colic "by contrary Operation," a gross scatological ridicule of physicians (III. v. 181). The ridicule is based on an eclectic parody in which, according to Miss Nicolson and Miss Mohler, "Swift has cleverly welded together two or more accounts and made a new combination." They go on to point out that "here Swift applies to Gulliver a series of experiments Shadwell had already popularized in the *Virtuoso* and implies, in addition, various later experiments performed by members of the Royal Society on the general subject of respiration and artificial respiration."[11] They further maintain that Swift's satire is also partly modeled on a contemporary account of "An extraordinary Effect of the Cholick" reported in *Philosophical Transactions* (1717).[12] The basic point in these parodies, therefore, is Swift's belief that when man fails to use his common sense and misdirects his intellectual resources, he cannot achieve any practical benefits from any endeavor he undertakes.

Besides scientific projectors and physicians, politicians also come under scatological attack in Gulliver's report of his visit to the school of political projectors. One of them proposes an improvement in the common defects of politicians through a medical approach, his reason being that "there is a strict universal Resemblance between the natural and the political Body" (III.vi.187). Physicians are to examine the senators and administer, according to the specific ailment of each patient, such medicines as "Lenitives, Aperitives, Abstersives, Corrosives, Restringents, Palliatives, Laxatives, Cephalalgicks, Ictericks, Apophlegmaticks, Acousticks" (III.vi.188). About half of these remedies are various kinds of laxatives. The connection between the medical and metaphorical associations in the scatological references to the politicians is hinted at in the description of the professor's qualifications. The professor "had very usefully employed his Studies in finding out effectual Remedies for all Diseases and Corruptions, to which the several Kinds of publick Administration are subject by the Vices or Infirmities of those who govern, as well as by the Licentiousness of those who are to obey" (III.vi.187). "Diseases and infirmities" (physical defects) are coupled with "corruptions and vices" (moral defects). Medically the failure of the politicians to "beget Unanimity, shorten Debates . . . curb the Petulancy of the Young . . . correct the Positiveness of the Old; rouze the Stupid, and damp the Pert" is attributed to their maladies (III.vi.188); metaphorically, however, these things are seen as manifestations of moral defects.

Another professor has a theory of "discovering Plots and Conspiracies against the Government" through medical uses of scatology, by an analysis and interpretation of the faeces of those persons suspected of plotting against the government.

> He advised great Statesmen to examine into the Dyet of all suspected Persons; their Times of eating; upon which Side they lay in Bed; with which Hand they wiped their Posteriors; to take a strict View of their Excrements, and from the Colour, the Odour, the Taste, the Consistence, the Crudeness, or Maturity of Digestion, form a Judgment of their Thoughts and Designs: Because Men are never so serious, thoughtful, and intent, as when they are at Stool; which he found by frequent Experiment: For in such Conjunctures, when he used merely as a Trial to consider which was the best Way of murdering the King, his Ordure would have a Tincture of Green; but quite different when he thought only of raising an Insurrection, or burning the Metropolis. (III.vi.190)

Politics no longer requires good morals and great abilities, or either of these qualities. Politics is lowered to the level of crude divination by consulting bowels of beasts as practised by the Greeks and Romans.[13]

There is a good deal of humor in these scatological passages, but the humor is obviously employed as a means of ridicule. The proposal to cure diseases (many of them disorders of the bowels) suffered by senators to "beget Unanimity, shorten Debates," etc., degrades politics to a matter of quackery, having nothing to do with the judgment of the senators, merits of the issues under consideration, or the common good of the people the senate is supposed to serve. Likewise, the offensive scheme of discovering conspiracies against the government by examining the faeces of the suspected persons suggests, though in an extravagantly humorous manner, the odious level politicians might stoop to in order to maintain their power. Even if such a scheme were practicable, the result of carrying out this scheme would only be disastrous to their reputation, for by handling excrements they would be reduced to a kind of gold-finder.[14] Not surprisingly some of the metaphors Swift suggests for politicians are scatological, connoting moral corruption and contempt; for example, a close stool for a privy council, a chamber pot for a committee of grandees, and a sink for a court (III.vi.191).

The exaggerated ridicule of the politicians reappears in Book IV of the *Travels,* where through scatology Swift emphasizes some despicable traits found in certain kinds of politicians; the Houyhnhnm master's explanation to Gulliver of the kind of Yahoos who become their leaders is an example. Gulliver recalls that according to his master "in most Herds [of Yahoos] there was a Sort of ruling *Yahoo,* (as among us there is generally some leading or principal Stag in a Park) who was always more *deformed* in Body, and *mischievous in Disposition,* than any of the rest" (IV.vii.262). It is, however, the description of the favorite that presents a loathsome image of sycophants found in any court:

> this *Leader* had usually a Favourite as *like himself* as he could get, whose Employment was to *lick his Master's feet and Posteriors, and drive the Female* Yahoos *to his Kennel;* for which he was now and then rewarded with a Piece of Ass's Flesh. This *Favourite* is hated by the whole Herd; and therefore to protect himself, keeps always *near the Person of his Leader*. He usually continues in Office till a worse can be found; but the very Moment he is discarded, his Successor, at the Head of all the *Yahoos* in that District, Young and Old, Male and Female, come in a Body, and discharge their Excrements upon him from Head to Foot.
>
> (IV.vii.262-63)

Gulliver adds, "But how far this might be applicable to our *Courts* and *Favourites,* and *Ministers of State,* my Master said I could best determine." This description is conventional in making physical deformity a metaphor of moral deformity and befoulment with excrement a figurative image of moral depravity. The image of licking posteriors at once reduces the leader and his minion to the lowest creatures on the moral scale. Appropriately enough the discarded minion is condemned by his enemies in an onslaught of excrements, the vilest expression of contempt fit for a vile creature. While all of these scatological references to and treatment of politicians are a devastating ridicule in themselves, they also underscore and reinforce Swift's non-scatological satire of politicians throughout the *Travels.* One of the nicest non-scatological expressions of his general attitude toward politicians and "the Art of Government" appears in Gulliver's account of the Brobdingnagian king's political naiveté:

> For, I remember very well, in a Discourse one Day with the King; when I happened to say, there were several thousand Books among us written upon the *Art of Government;* it gave him (directly contrary to my Intention) a very mean Opinion of our Understandings. He professed both to abominate and despise all *Mystery, Refinement,* and *Intrigue,* either in a Prince or a Minister. . . . He confined the Knowledge of governing within very *narrow Bounds;* to common Sense and Reason, to Justice and Lenity, to the Speedy Determination of Civil and criminal Causes. . . . And, he gave it for his Opinion; that whoever could make two Ears of Corn, or two Blades of Grass to grow upon a Spot of Ground where only one grew before; would deserve better of Mankind, and do more essential Service to his Country, than the whole Race of Politicians put together.[15]
>
> (II.vii.135-36)

In Book IV, Swift also employs scatology in denouncing repletion as an odious vice. In Gulliver's account of European civilization to his Houyhnhnm master we note a scatological description of a basic theory and cure of diseases. Gulliver explains how physicians approach various diseases:

> Their Fundamental is, that all Diseases arise from *Repletion;* from whence they conclude, that a great *Evacuation* of the Body is necessary, either through the natural Passage, or upwards at the Mouth. Their next Business is, from Herbs, Minerals, Gums, Oyls, Shells, Salts, Juices, Sea-weed, Excrements, Barks of Trees, Serpents, Toads, Frogs, Spiders, dead Mens Flesh and Bones, Birds, Beasts and Fishes, to form a Composition for Smell and Taste the most abominable, nauseous and detestable, that they can possibly contrive, which the Stomach immediately rejects with Loathing: And this they call a *Vomit.* Or else from the same Store-house, with some other poysonous Additions, they command us to take in at the Orifice *above* or *below,* (just as the Physician then happens to be disposed) a Medicine equally annoying and disgustful to the Bowels; which relaxing the Belly, drives down all before it: And this they call a *Purge,* or a *Clyster.* For Nature (as the Physicians alledge) having intended the superior anterior Orifice only for the *Intromission* of Solids and Liquids, and the inferior Posterior for Ejection; these Artists ingeniously considering that in all Diseases Nature is forced out of her Seat; therefore to replace her in it, the Body must be treated in a Manner directly contrary, by interchanging the Use of each Orifice; forcing Solids and Liquids in at the *Anus,* and making Evacuations at the Mouth.
>
> (IV.vi.253-54)

This satire is directed not only against quacks who treat all diseases alike, but also against a much more important target of Swift's attack—repletion, a vice associated with failure of reason. Only men and Yahoos, creatures of imperfect reason or non-reason, are subject to this vice. When Gulliver, like his Houyhnhnm master, takes only enough simple food to satisfy his natural want, he remains healthy (Houyhnhnms do not suffer from malnutrition or disease). How odious this vice appears to Swift may be seen by the repulsive cures he suggests.

Gulliver notes that Houyhnhnms cure Yahoos' maladies of repletion by forcing them to take a laxative, "a Mixture of *their own Dung* and *Urine,*" and recommends this measure to his audience "for the publick Good, as an admirable Specifick against all Diseases produced by Repletion" (IV.vii.262). For when a man suffers from this vice, he is no better than the brute Yahoo, a mindless creature. Like Dante, Swift would have such a man wallow in the mire of his loathsome vice "in a Manner directly contrary" to that normally accorded to a reasonable being.

The most important use Swift makes of scatology in Book IV, however, is his conception of the Yahoo, because Swift's attack on human pride hinges on his degrading man below the level of the Yahoo. The main sources of man's pride are his body and mind, which he believes set him above and apart from all other earthly creatures. Of the three, the Houyhnhnm stands at the apex as a creature "naturally disposed to every Virtue, wholly governed by Reason" (IV.ix.273). At the other extreme of the scale stands the Yahoo, a brute devoid of reason. If our impression of the Houyhnhnm through the eyes of Gulliver is primarily rational and virtuous, our impression of the Yahoo is at once physical. If the Houyhnhnms impress Gulliver as superhuman in rationality, the Yahoos strike Gulliver as subhuman in physical appearance. They are so ugly that Gulliver concludes upon his initial observation that "Upon the whole, I never beheld in all my Travels so disagreeable an Animal, or one against which I naturally conceived so strong an Antipathy" (IV.i.223-24). Above all, the Yahoos are excremental. A baby Yahoo defecates all over Gulliver almost by instinct as he dandles it (IV.viii.266). Even more shocking to Gulliver is his first encounter with Yahoos; in one of the filthiest scenes in the *Travels* a herd of them shower him with their excrements (IV.i.224).[16]

This excremental shower is similar to the vile treatment given to the fallen Yahoo favorite (IV.vii.263), and in the context of the subsequent lowering of Gulliver physically to the level of the Yahoos and morally below them, this act is symbolic of Gulliver's identification as a depraved Yahoo. Their mutual hostility only confirms their basic common identity, for the Yahoos (according to the Houyhnhnm) were "known to hate one another more than they did any different Species of Animals; and the Reason usually assigned, was, the Odiousness of their own Shapes, which all could see in the rest, but not in themselves" (IV.vii.260). The physical relationship between the two is carefully prepared by explicit and suggestive comparisons of bodily characteristics. Gulliver's introduction to the Yahoos begins with his discovery of the Yahoos' footprints, which he takes for "many Tracks of human Feet" (IV.i.223). A little later when he secretly observes Yahoos, Gulliver notes such apparently nonhuman characteristics as their deformed shapes, strong claws with hooked points, and hairy backs. Significantly enough, however, he also notes that "The Hair of both Sexes was of several Colours, brown, red, black and yellow" (IV.i.223). The connection is more pointedly made when the Houyhnhnm master comments that among the Yahoos "the *Red-haired* of both Sexes are more libidinous and mischievous than the rest, whom yet they much exceed in Strength and Activity" (IV.viii.266). Still later standing side by side with a Yahoo at the bidding of his Houyhnhnm master who studies both of them, Gulliver recognizes to his "Horror and Astonishment . . . a perfect human Figure" in the Yahoo (IV.ii.229-30). The physical equation is made beyond doubt when a female Yahoo spies on naked Gulliver and takes him for a Yahoo (IV.viii.267).

Swift's attack on man's pride in his mind, though not rendered in scatological terms, stems from downgrading Gulliver's pride in his body. Having exposed the basic similarities of the human body to the Yahoo, Swift strips the human mind of its claim to superiority by baring its defects. The limitations of the human mind are obvious when compared to the mind of the Houyhnhnm to whom (Gulliver explains) reason is not "a Point problematical as with us, where Men can argue with Plausibility on both Sides of a Question" (IV.viii.267). On the other hand, one thing that does distinguish Gulliver from the Yahoos is (in the Houyhnhnm's words) "Appearances of Reason" (IV. iii.234), for which the Houyhnhnms treat Gulliver as an advanced Yahoo. Yet it turns out that in the Houyhnhnms' eyes man fares much worse than the Yahoos because of his rational power.

A blistering indictment of man's unwarranted pride in his mind follows Gulliver's account to his Houyhnhnm master of the mores, institutions, and affairs of his country and of Europe. He enumerates the many malpractices among lawyers and physicians, political intrigues at court, the "Luxury and Intemperance of the Males, and the Vanity of the Females" (IV.vi.252). He also talks of revolutions, mercenaries, causes of wars, various kinds of weapons, tactics, and enormous casualties in battles, causing in the Houyhnhnm "a Disturbance in his Mind, to which he was wholly a Stranger before" (IV.v.248). The account of these terrible acts of mutual destruction motivated by greed or pride (such as differences of opinions on trivial matters) forces the Houyhnhnm to condemn and degrade man morally to a level below the Yahoos. Using a Baconian simile which compares human reason to a false mirror that reflects a distorted image, the Houyhnhnm declares in one of the most telling denunciations in the *Travels* that

> although he hated the *Yahoos* of this Country, yet he no more blamed them for their odious Qualities, than he did a *Gnnayh* (a Bird of Prey) for its Cruelty, or a sharp Stone for cutting his Hoof. But, when a Creature pretending to Reason, could be capable of such Enormities, he dreaded lest the Corruption of that Faculty might be worse than Brutality itself. He seemed therefore confident, that instead of Reason, we were only possessed of some Quality fitted to increase our natural Vices; as the Reflection from a troubled Stream returns the Image of an ill-shapen Body, not only *larger,* but more *distorted.*
>
> (IV.v.248)

Because his point of view is that of a European accustomed to a history of conquests, Gulliver does not see that in his account of wars and the invention of weapons he has unwittingly testified to man's propensity to abuse his reason for destructive ends. Strictly examined, Gulliver's account of European history is, of course, unbalanced in its omission of more positive progress, as seen in Swift's ironical self-defense, when he has Gulliver confess that "it is now some Comfort to reflect, that in what I said of my Countrymen, I *extenuated* their Faults as much as I durst before so strict an Examiner; and upon every Article, gave as *favourable* a Turn as the Matter would bear" (IV.vii. 258-59). At the same time, however, his account is not totally false; it only concentrates on recognizable human vices, though in an exaggerated manner. The justice of the Houyhnhnm's condemnation is evident when we realize that the particular vices Gulliver enumerates are peculiarly human vices engendered by greed, vanity, pride, or all of these, cultivated by human intelligence. It seems that to be intelligent in a human sense means to be evil. If Gulliver sees his rational capacity as his unique virtue, the Houyhnhnm suggests that he is much the worse for his abuse of this capacity. Hence the Houyhnhnm degrades mankind morally far below the level of the Yahoos, the brutes incapable of moral judgment or reason. He concludes that man made no better use of his "small Pittance of *Reason*" than to "aggrevate our *natural* Corruptions, and to acquire new ones which Nature had not given us" (IV.vii.259). In the Houyhnhnm's denunciation of "man's natural propensity towards evil"[17] and his inhumanity to one another through misuse of reason, we are made to feel that moral odiousness is far worse than physical odiousness.

Though not rendered in explicit scatology, Swift's attack on the evils of the human mind is not wholly free of scatological associations. For the Houyhnhnm's denunciation is a part of Swift's overall attack on the corruption and waste of the human mind. War and its attendant activities, including the invention of weapons, are one visible form of waste of intellectual endeavor and human resources on a massive scale. The way many lawyers and politicians distort the truth for personal gain is also a form of moral and intellectual corruption. The idea of waste and corruption in itself suggests figurative association with *skata.* This association becomes clearer when we recall the Academy of Lagado where, as we have seen, the myopic projectors suffer from some of the crudest scatology in the *Travels.*

Swift extends his attack on man's moral and intellectual degeneration in more readily discernible scatological associations in the Houyhnhnm's observation of the Yahoos in order to note the "Parity" in the character of the Yahoo and man (IV.vii.262). More specifically, Swift hints at man's natural depravity by parity with the Yahoo and the corruption of the human mind by disparity with the Houyhnhnm. This means that we must translate Yahoo behavior into corresponding human manifestations whenever the connection between the two is pointed out or hinted at. This also means that because Swift readily exploits possibilities of figurative and connotative meanings of words useful to his purposes, we must look for satiric or ironic innuendoes whenever we suspect such a possibility. On the whole, however, Swift helps us with obvious clues so that we can easily see the particular target he has in mind. The filthy character of the Yahoo leader and his favorite, for example, forges an instant link with corrupt statesmen and their lackeys. Sometimes, however, the similarity between the Yahoo and man is hinted at subtly. I refer to what Gulliver might call another instance of the Houyhnhnm's "malicious Insinuation," when the master comments on the Yahoos' "strange Disposition to Nastiness and Dirt," which (Gulliver says) the master "had not observed me to mention, or at least very slightly" in Gulliver's account of human character (IV.vii.263). Since in the literal sense "Nastiness and Dirt" mean dirty things such as filth, grime, and muck, the Houyhnhnm's comment strikes us as wholly irrelevant to human habits.[18] On the other hand, if in the metaphorical sense the two words refer to morally offensive and unclean things, the Houyhnhnm's observation is generally applicable to human character. Swift does not let this implication remain vague, however. Gulliver recalls:

> I could have easily vindicated human Kind from the Imputation of Singularity upon the last Article [Yahoos' "strange Disposition to Nastiness and Dirt"], if there had been any *Swine* in that Country . . . which although it may be a *sweeter Quadruped* than a *Yahoo,* cannot I humbly conceive in Justice pretend to more Cleanliness; and so his Honour himself must have owned, if he had seen their filthy Way of feeding, and their Custom of wallowing and sleeping in the Mud.
>
> (IV.vii.263)

If in the literal sense, the word "sweeter" refers to the sense of smell, the passage notes that though the swine may smell less offensive, it is still a filthier animal than the Yahoo. If this is one meaning, the implication of the passage is not at all consoling, for the notion of defending man's cleanliness by comparing it to a swine is classifying man in the category of a swine. We suspect figurative possibilities and twisting of irony, however, in the connotations of certain words. The "swine," of course, is a metaphor for a greedy man, a man of "undistinguishing Appetite" (IV.vii.261).[19] "Sweeter," then, would mean—in its ironic reference to swine—odious, degenerate, and even hateful (the opposite of "fragrant," "fresh," and "beloved" in the non-ironic sense). "Wallowing" suggests sensuality, self-indulgence, and excess, while "mud" (which in its literal reference is excremental) connotes corruption. On the figurative level, therefore, the passage illustrates the vices of sensuality, corruption, and repletion—all associated with failure of reason. If this is another meaning, the implication of the passage is equally satirical, for those guilty of such swinish vices are reduced to a level lower than the Yahoos.

This ready exploitation of the literal and figurative meanings of words and references serves Swift well in reminding man of the imperfections of his body and mind, especially through the idea of correspondence between "outside and inside."[20] "Outside" refers to things that appeal to our senses, including the sense of smell; "inside" refers to things hidden beneath the surface, including nonphysical qualities, such as moral corruption. The odious body of the Yahoo, for example, reflects his odious vices. Thus the Houyhnhnm characterizes the Yahoo dispositions as having "odious Qualities" (IV.v.248). For the same reason the Houyhnhnms, who object to the Yahoos' "offensive Smell," find their dispositions "evil" (IV.ix.272). Swift relates man to the Yahoo by smell (outside) and hints at parity in their character (inside). Body odor in itself is not necessarily scatological, but with the Yahoo it is definitely associated with *skata*. We think at once of the Yahoos' excremental shower on Gulliver. Moreover, Gulliver describes the smell of the baby Yahoo to be "very rank, and the Stink was somewhat between a *Weasel* and a *Fox*, but much more disagreeable." The physical relationship between the Yahoo and man is more insistently suggested in Gulliver's defilement by the same infant Yahoo who "voided its filthy Excrements of a yellow liquid Substance, all over my Cloaths" (IV.viii.266).

Furthermore, in the *Travels* ordinarily quasi-scatological words like "stink," which Gulliver mentions above, acquire unmistakable scatological associations when employed in scatological situations. We may refer, for example, to Gulliver's visit to the Academy of Lagado and his "being almost overcome with a horrible Stink" of the room where the projector carries out an excremental undertaking of extracting food (III.v.179). Thus, when Gulliver returns to human society and finds the smell of men offensive, Swift is hinting at the essential Yahoo nature in man and is reminding us of our "*natural* Corruptions" (outside and inside again), which the Houyhnhnm master has earlier spoken of when he condemned the human mind that invents evil things like weapons of massive destruction. That this is not a casual or passing notion may be seen in several references to men's offensive smell. Walking in the streets of Lisbon, Gulliver is forced to keep his "Nose well stopped with Rue, or sometimes with Tobacco" (IV.xi. 288), as though he were afraid of being contaminated by a plague through human contact.[21] Later at the reunion with his family, he refers to human kind as that "odious Animal" (IV.xi.289), the same phrase he used earlier in the Houyhnhnmland in referring to the Yahoo (IV.iii.237). Some five years later he still finds human beings, including his wife, odious animals: ". . . the Smell of a *Yahoo* continuing very offensive, I always keep my Nose stopt with Rue, Lavender, or Tobacco-Leaves" (IV.xii.295).

It is natural, therefore, that scatology is associated with irrational or evil beings like Yahoo and man; it is likewise natural that it is not associated with rational or virtuous beings like the Houyhnhnms and the Brobdingnagian king. While scatology does not appear in the personal references to the Lilliputian king, it applies to him indirectly when Gulliver relieves himself in the temple-house just before the king's arrival there for their first meeting. We have also seen Gulliver's offense to the queen by making water at the palace. In the case of intellectually degenerate Laputians, the satirical description of their persons ("Their Heads were all reclined either to the Right, or the Left . . ." [III.ii.159]) is completed by the reference to the blown bladder which their servants flap to their mouths and ears to arouse their attention. One exception seems to be the Portuguese captain and his crew, who are among the small number of good men in the *Travels*. Gulliver finds the captain "a very courteous and generous Person" and calls his crew "honest Portuguese." Nevertheless, in their company Gulliver was "ready to faint at the very Smell" of them (IV.xi.286).

The implications of the many scatological associations with the Yahoo, I suggest, are directly related to Swift's ideas about human nature. One implication is that man's basic Yahoo nature, in the eyes of the Houyhnhnm, is tainted with natural vices and corruption. Deane Swift (Swift's relative and one of his eighteenth-century biographers), Louis A. Landa, and Roland M. Frye have pointed out that this idea of the natural depravity of human nature is an orthodox Christian concept that underlies the last voyage.[22] Corollary implications are that "even good Yahoos are Yahoos"[23] and that "man is never free of the limitations of his nature."[24] This means that in order to rise above his Yahoo nature, man must constantly be aware of it and control it.

Swift's idea of the natural depravity of human nature is developed elsewhere in the *Travels* in non-scatological terms through repeated references to human degeneration. Swift suggests that the whole human race has steadily degenerated, presumably since the Fall.[25] Gulliver describes the idealistic social and political institutions of Lilliput, but adds in the same breath that "I would only be understood to mean the original Institutions, and not the most scandalous Corruptions into which these People are fallen by the degenerate Nature of Man" (I.vi.60). A similar idea is hinted at in Gulliver's account of the Brobdingnagians, who, according to one of their moralists, are descendants of much larger ancestors, since "Nature was degenerated in these latter declining Ages of the World, and could now produce only small abortive Births in Comparison of those in ancient Times" (II.vii.137). The correspondence of outside and inside applies here too; physical degeneration takes place simultaneously with moral degeneration. The virtuous King notwithstanding, Brobdingnagians have beggars and criminals among them and they maintain militia to protect them against civil strife, "For, in the Course of many Ages they have been troubled with the same Disease, to which the whole Race of Mankind is Subject; the Nobility often contending for Power, the People for Liberty, and the King for absolute Dominion" (II.vii.138). The human race itself is viewed in a steadily degenerative spiral. Gulliver's visit with the spirits of the ancient poets and philosophers (Homer, Socrates), statesmen and soldiers (Caesar, Brutus), and lowly "*English* Yeomen of the old Stamp" clearly illustrates man's physical, intellectual, and moral degeneration accompanied by avarice (especially of money), luxury (especially of diet), and diseases (especially pox) (III. vii-viii.195-202). By drawing our attention repeatedly to this idea of steady human degeneration and the natural depravity of human nature, Swift seems to suggest broadly that man must realize that he is degenerate in order to strive for moral regeneration. He also suggests that man's natural corruption does not allow him a moment of self-complacency.

When we consider the function of scatology in the *Travels* as a whole, we do not find any major instance of misuse or wasting of the device for its own sake. In any instance scatology ultimately contributes to satiric purposes. This generalization applies even to the instances of Gulliver's acts of relieving himself in the first two voyages, where the local and immediate effects are, as we have seen, mainly humorous. In the end, however, I do not think that these episodes are irrelevant to Swift's satire of mankind. We sense a deliberate lowering of Gulliver's stature and dignity; we feel invited, as it were, to laugh at Gulliver (and even at Swift himself). At the same time, however, we are disarmingly introduced to scatology in a humorous manner. This is a subtle manipulation of our initial reaction to scatology in the *Travels* on the part of Swift,[26] because there is a shift in tone and manner in the use of scatology in the last two voyages—from humor to shock and disgust. (T.S. Eliot was right to praise Swift as "the great master of disgust.")[27] When the narrative takes us to the Academy of Lagado and the Houyhnhnmland, we no longer laugh at Gulliver, who is now more often a reporter than a major actor in excremental situations. The function of scatology becomes pointedly satiric, and instead of being amused we are nauseated by crude scatology. It is as though in the first two voyages we are given a chance to overcome our sense of revulsion to scatology; after scatology has been introduced in a humorous manner at Gulliver's (and Swift's) expense and our defenses are relaxed, Swift in the last two voyages concentrates on ugly scatological details for intense satiric effects that might earlier have been too sudden or shocking. To define the pattern in another way, scatology goes from the humorous to the satiric as the probing of the nature of man goes from outward to inward through the four voyages. Insofar as he is simply "homo," we are invited to laugh at him tolerantly, especially as he tries to conceal his similarity to other animals or overcome his sense of shame concerning his anality. But as he begins to qualify the "homo" by "rationis," his failure to define and practice cleanliness becomes a moral matter and is castigated, not smiled at.

Swift closes the book, however, not with an ugly shock, but with a subtle hint, whose implication is no less disconcerting for being less obviously scatological. When Gulliver stuffs his nose with tobacco, we do not miss the comic irony of his action, nor do we overlook the underlying point that with all the physical, intellectual, and moral limitations of man, we too are odious, though like Gulliver we may tend to discover the Yahoo in others but not in ourselves.

Conclusion

Critics from Swift's time to the present have claimed that he was obsessed with excrement. Many of these critics are hygienists who find any scatology not only unsavory but also inhuman.[1] Though I have encountered much censure of Swift for his employment of scatology as a literary device, I have not seen a similar protest against Dante for his detailed description of the excremental inferno or against Rabelais for his copious account of the excremental adventures of his giant heroes. Dante is not questioned because he is recognized as moral; Rabelais is spared because he is considered humanistic. Swift is as moral and as humanistic as either of his illustrious predecessors. That Swift's writings are moral in character is evident from the fact that he never indulges in prurience or scato-erotic humor and that he seldom uses scatology for solely meretricious reasons. Even in predominantly humorous pieces, such as the verse-riddles on the privy and posteriors, his use of scatology usually accompanies, even if in an oblique manner, some satiric innuendo.

The notoriety connected with Swift's scatological writings, I believe, stems from the reader's failure to appreciate the moral and humanistic character of his scatology, in particular his scatological humor, in which he may seem to invite only laughter at the expense of our anality. Often Swift not only provokes our boisterous laughter, but also forces our acceptance of the truth of our animal nature so that we may not be ashamed of our true selves, including our inescapable anality. In this respect Swift is a true humanist who attempts to free us from our prejudices and the futile denial of our basic nature; the more heartily we can laugh by means of scatological humor, the more completely we accept ourselves as mortal beings. For such a purpose a true humanist does not shy away from scatology. On the contrary, he is almost obligated to use it.

In his humorous reference to our anality, Swift never takes a self-righteous or superior attitude toward his subject or maintains an antiseptic distance from it. Instead, he identifies himself with the victim of his humor so that we may all share the humor as equals. When Gulliver describes how he met the call of nature in that delicate kingdom where everything human is magnified in all its details, we also laugh at Swift and through him at ourselves. By allowing us to laugh at him as well as at Gulliver, Swift hints that he is not above us and that what he says about Gulliver and mankind applies to the author as well. In this sense Swift's scatological humor is moral as well as funny, perhaps the more moral for being funny, because such laughter is truly "an affirmation of shared values."[2] If we cannot laugh at our anality and accept ourselves as mortal beings, we may very well—like the neurotic Cassinus—lose our wits so that we see walking jakes everywhere. Or, we may become cynical vulgarians like Strephon and make no attempt to be decent.

Though Swift is traditional in his use of scatology as a satiric device, he is unique in English literature in the way he uses scatology as a weapon of attack against major targets. In general, while others resort to scatology intermittently, Swift—without squeamish apology—turns it into a formidable weapon in a consistent attack. If he does apologize, it is to capitalize on our sense of shame concerning our animal body. No other English satirist employs this device with so much flexibility or force. His full exploitation of the various possibilities of scatology to serve his diverse purposes is a measure of his artistic skill. To cite specific functions, Swift employs human excrement as a symbol for man's physical and moral corruptions. The use of excrement as a metaphor for moral corruption and spiritual degeneration is a conventional idea which Swift inherits. From this basic idea he derives further associations, so that excrement becomes a complex symbol whose particular meaning is determined in its particular context. While we may discern various conventional associations in Swift's uses of this symbol, we may also recognize that it is not merely an eclectic symbol, but a Swiftian symbol which gains in force because of its multiple meanings. Certainly no other major satirist, at least in the English language, derives such diverse associations from this symbol as Swift does.

To recapitulate, we have noted that in Swift's writings excrement and related matter such as flatulency and privy are employed as figures of speech for money and the Bank, vices of language and mind, religious fanaticism, the natural depravity of man, man's animal nature and limitations, mortality and humanity.

In closing our discussion, we may briefly consider the scatological elements in *A Panegyrick on the D--n* (1730), recently condemned for its "crude latrine humour"[3] and attacked as "Swift's only scatological poem that seems in any sense coprophilous."[4] The scatological passages pertain to Swift's speculation (through the persona of Lady Acheson, his hostess at a country estate in Northern Ireland) on the origin of our shame concerning human excrement. Swift sees our shameful association with excrement as a reflection of man's gradual moral degeneration engendered by our growing sense of greed and pride. He observes that in the mythical ages "When *Saturn* rul'd the Skies alone,/ That *golden* Age, to *Gold* unknown" (ll. 233-34), man in the state of prelapsarian innocence had no "Altars fix't beneath" (l. 232) for "Goddess *Cloacine,*" no craving for wealth, and no awareness of shame concerning his excrement. But when "usurping *Jove*" took over Saturn's empire "*Gluttony* with greasy paws" appeared on the scene and "Taught harmless Man to cram and stuff" (l. 262) and "Confin'd Thee Goddess to a Cell" (l. 270). It is significant that Jove "usurps" Saturn; that is, Jove, motivated by greed, takes what is not properly his. Swift develops the concept that greed and pride are the origin of moral degeneration and our attendant shame concerning human anality. Gluttony prompts man to abandon a simple diet for an elaborate one and instills in man the notion of luxury and sloth so that he separates himself from his original abode. Men now in

> . . . Cells and Vaults obscene
> Present a Sacrifice unclean;
> From whence unsav'ry Vapours rose,
> Offensive to thy [Cloacine's] nicer Nose.
> (ll. 283-86)

The symbolic progression from innocence to experience may be seen in the implication that the vaults are described as "obscene" and excrement "unclean" and "offensive." The vaults are a visible symbol of man's willful separation from nature and an assertion of his individual identity, while his excrement, now turned offensive in smell, is a symbol of his physical and moral degeneration. In this context excrement is a concrete sign of man's degeneration: the more corrupt he is in body and mind, the more unclean his excrement, therefore the more shameful to man as he strives to rise above his humble origin. We may also recall the conventional metaphor of excrement for money, as well as Swift's satire of the Bank, and consider the possibility of a figurative allusion to man's gradual moral degeneration through his greed and through his hoarding of money. It is partly man's amassing of the offerings for Cloacine that makes his sacrifice so vile. Likewise, cramming and stuffing corrupt man and make him susceptible to Sloth, Dropsy, Gout, Asthma, Ease, and Wealth, all offsprings of Gluttony. Man becomes infected with pride based on wealth and social distinction, while remaining in body the same as he ever was so that he must still be a follower of Cloacine whether on "Earthen Ware" (l. 295) or "Silver Base" (l. 298). The contrast between the act of necessity as an open deed in our state of innocence and as a secretive deed in our state of advancement also recalls for us the metaphor of excrement for sin. If man became more vile in body and mind as he became more sinful, offensive excrement is a symbol of his spiritual fall.

The charge of obscenity against Swift, because of his uses of scatology, is ironic because he devoted a large part of his career to destroying what he regarded as really obscene—human pride and greed, man's misuses of his reason, man's inhumanity to his fellowmen. In an age of reason and enlightenment when men felt confident of their ability to solve various problems through human intelligence and also optimistic of continual progress, Swift stands out as an exceptional critic of man's smug self-complacency in his inhumane world. We would be ignorant to condemn Swift solely because of his uses of scatology. The least we should do is to recognize the legitimacy and the neutral character of scatology as a literary device and to consider what purposes this device serves in a given work. If one denounces Swift for his use of this device, even for didactic purposes, because the reader simply does not like scatology and because (he may argue) Swift did not have to resort to it, at least he should not single out Swift but denounce others as well, including Dante. And if one condemns Swift for his scatological humor, he should do so out of his own personal dislike of it and not out of his mistaken notion that Swift is unique in indulging in this kind of humor, which is a minor but a distinct genre that goes back at least as far as the comedies of Aristophanes.

In fact, Swift's scatological humor is not nearly so excremental as some of the stercoraceous pieces we have seen. Anyone who hurls a charge of filth against Swift should examine the function of scatology in Swift's works within the context of a long literary tradition of scatology. He may then see that his charge is not valid in the light of literary facts.

Notes

INTRODUCTION

1 Reid B. Sinclair's unpublished dissertation, " 'What the World Calls Obscene': Swift's 'Ugly' Verse and the Satiric Tradition" (Vanderbilt University, 1965), takes up this topic, but the scope of this study is limited to Swift's poetry, and the "ugly" elements it discusses include "obscene" as well as scatological elements. To my knowledge, this is the first extended study on the topic. More recently, Donald Greene concentrates on the scatological elements in his provocative essay, "On Swift's 'Scatological' Poems" (*Sewanee Review,* LXXV [1967], 672-89).

2 *The Lives of the Most Eminent Poets* (London, 1816), III, 45.

3 "On Wit and Humour," Lecture IX, *Miscellaneous Criticism,* ed. T. M. Raysor (Cambridge, Mass., 1936), p. 114.

4 *History of English Literature,* tr. H. Van Laun (New York, 1965), III, 237.

5 "Swift," *Do What You Will* (London, 1936), p. 73.

6 Ibid., p. 78.

7 *Jonathan Swift* (New York, 1955).

8 *English Literature in the Early Eighteenth Century* (Oxford, 1964), p. 462.

9 "The scene is always crowded, disorderly, grotesque; the satirist, in those satires where he appears, is always indignant, dedicated to truth, pessimistic, and caught in a series of unpleasant contradictions incumbent on practicing his trade; the plot always takes the pattern of purpose followed by passion, but fails to develop beyond this point," *The Cankered Muse* (New Haven, 1959), p. 35.

10 Worcester, for example, declares that "the content of satire is criticism," *The Art of Satire* (Cambridge, Mass., 1940), p. 16. Ellen Douglas Leyburn in *Satiric Allegory* (New Haven, 1956) maintains that in satire "there is always a judgment of faults" (p. 7). This notion of satire as primarily an attack or criticism is also advanced by John M. Bullitt in *Jonathan Swift and the Anatomy of Satire*

(Cambridge, Mass., 1953): "Whether good or bad, general or particular, true or false, savage or humorous, prosaic or poetic—any literary attack upon the vice or folly of men and manners may be contained under the general word satire" (p. 39).

CHAPTER 1

1 *The Clouds,* in *Aristophanes,* tr. Benjamin Bickley Rogers, Loeb Classical Library (London, 1924), I, 275.

2 In *The Peace* (421 B.C.) Aristophanes employs scatology as a means of denouncing warmongers like Cleon and the armorers. The foulest figure is the enormous dung beetle. Trygaeus, the Athenian patriot and the hero of the play, rides on the beetle to heaven in search of the goddess Peace. The beetle is described as "a most stinking, foul, voracious brute" (p. 7) and the feeding of the beetle is suggested as a skit "aimed at Cleon,/ It eats the muck" so "shamelessly" (p. 9). The Chorus alludes to Cleon in the figure of a monster "whose hinder parts like a furnace appeared" (p. 71).

With the restoration of peace, Trygaeus sarcastically remarks to the bankrupt armorers that the splendid habergeon will now "do superbly for my chamber-pan" (p. 113) and that the helmets are "just the things" for Egyptians to "measure physic in" (i.e., "a strong purge," p. 115 and n.a). The association of Cleon with the beetle is particularly noteworthy, for through this association Aristophanes insinuates that the character of Cleon is odious. Just as the beetle gorges on its filthy food, by implication Cleon is seen as thriving on the filthy lucre of the war. (The page numbers refer to those in *The Peace,* in *Aristophanes,* tr. Rogers, Loeb Classical Library [London, 1924], II.)

3 *Satires,* I. x. 66, *The Satires and Epistles of Horace,* tr. Smith Palmer Bovie (Chicago, 1959), p. 80. Cf. Martial, XII. 94.7: "I venture satire: you strain to be a Lucilius" ("audemus saturas: Lucilius esse laboras").

4 Horace declares that

> The poets Cratinus, Eupolis, and Aristophanes,
> And the others who wrote Old Comedy, used to name names:
> They felt perfectly free to describe the rascal and thief
> As a rascally thief, the lecher as lecher, the cutthroat,
> Or anyone with a bad name, as deserving his real
> Reputation. Lucilius' satire distinctly derives
> From these writers; he followed them closely, only in meter
> And form differing from them.

(*Satires,* I.iv.1-7, tr. Bovie, p. 52. Of the works of Cratinus, Eupolis, and Aristophanes, only those of Aristophanes are extant.)

The *Satires of Horace,* as we know, are not remarkable for scatological elements. This does not mean that they are completely devoid of them. Scatology does occur in the Eighth Satire of Book One where Horace makes fun of the "witches/ Who stir up the souls of the living with potions and chants" (lines

19-20). Unlike Catullus, however, Horace employs scatology for humorous ridicule and not for harsh diatribe.

5 E. H. Warmington, "Introduction," *Remains of Old Latin,* tr. Warmington, Loeb Classical Library, III (Cambridge, Mass., 1938), xx. For a discussion of Lucilius' satires, see C. A. Van Rooy's *Studies in Classical Satire and Related Literary Theory* (Leiden, 1965), pp. 51-55.

6 Paulus notes that " 'Bubinare' means to defile with the blood from women's monthly flow" and that " 'Inbulbitare' means to defile with a boy's dung" (*Remains of Old Latin,* III, 385). Other examples include the following fragments: "She didn't *bring* him forth but from the hinder part she *sprawled* him forth" ("Non peperit, verum postica parte profudit") (pp. 36-37); "Would you reasonably believe that anyone here has made for the baths?" ("Hic tu apte credis quemquam latrina petisse?") (pp. 88-89); "who grows languid in the wash-bath" ("qui in latrina languet") (pp. 136-37); "What a dirty face he's got because he has thrown out of the camp all those fellows to a man like dung into the open" ("quam spurcust ore, quod omnes extra castra ut stercus foras eiecit ad unum") (pp. 136-37); "it may be worth while to pick out with the teeth gold from flame, food from filth" ("mordicus petere aurum e flamma expediat, e caeno cibum") (pp. 212-13); "If he has fouled his clothes with dirt, from this he unwittingly prompts great laughter and jeering" ("Si hic vestimenta elevit luto, ab eo risum magnum inprudens ac cachinnum subicit") (pp. 218-19); "I wetted all the bed and made messes on the skins" ("Perminxi lectum, inposui pedem pellibus labes") (pp. 386-87).

7 *The Poems of Catullus,* tr. Horace Gregory (New York, 1931), pp. 93, 95.

8 We also discover in Catullus a minor but important use of scatology to condemn mean language. In referring to bad writing, Catullus uses the term "cacata charta" (XXXVI, lines 1, 20), and in condemning a chatty tongue he suggests that the man might lick a rustic's posteriors and shoes ("ista cum lingua, si usus veniat tibi, possis/ culos et crepidas lingere carpatinas") (XCVIII, lines 3-4, *The Poems of Gaius Valerius Catullus,* ed. F. W. Cornish, in *Catullus, Tibullus and Pervigilium Veneris,* Loeb Classical Library [Cambridge, Mass., 1962], p. 170). Cf. Martial, I. 83; III. 28.

9 Of the other scatological examples, III. 78, 89; IV. 87 are more humorous than satirical in effect. Those containing a brief scatological reference for purposes of satire include III. 44; VI. 93; X. 14; XI. 98; XII. 32, 40, 48, 61.

10 *Martial: Epigrams,* tr. Walter C. A. Ker, Loeb Classical Library (London, 1919), I, 411. Cf. II. 42, 70.

11 English translation is by Hubert Creekmore, *The Satires of Juvenal,* Mentor Classics (New York, 1963). My Latin text for Juvenal is *Juvenal and Persius,* ed. G. G. Ramsay, Loeb Classical Library (London, 1940).

12 Juvenal's admiration for Lucilius may be inferred from his allusions to the earlier master (see lines 20, 151-54, 165-66, all in Satire One).

13 J. Wight Duff, *Roman Satire* (Berkeley, 1936), p. 162. Dryden in "A Discourse concerning the Original and Progress of Satire" (1693) makes a similar comment: "he [Juvenal] treats tyranny, and all the vices attending it, as

they deserve, with the utmost rigour . . ." (*Essays of John Dryden*, ed. W. P. Ker [New York, 1961], II, 86-87).

14 Elsewhere Juvenal encourages violating an Egyptian statue, which he suggests "With no fear of arrest, you may do even more than merely piss" ("cuius ad effigiem non tantum meiere fas est") (I. 131).

15. This technique of exposing the baser reality beneath a fine appearance is, of course, one of the fundamental methods all satirists use. It is a method Juvenal uses throughout his work. Lucilius seems to have been a master of this technique. Horace comments that Lucilius "stripped off the skin/ Wherein everyone flaunts his good looks in his neighbor's eyes/ While inwardly ugly . . ." (*Satires*, II. i. 62-65, tr. Bovie).

16 For a definitive account of the formal verse satire, see Mary Claire Randolph's "The Structural Design of the Formal Verse Satire," *Philogical Quarterly*, XXI (1942), 368-84. When Dante employs scatology outside *Inferno*, his purpose is the same—to reveal the foul nature of evil. In *Purgatorio*, Dante dreams of a siren whose stench (when Vergil bares her belly) awakens him (XIX. 31-33).

17 "Mud" in *Inferno* always carries a connotation, if not a denotation, of excrement. Dante's inferno is a vast torture chamber full of "the stynkynge ordure of synne" (I borrow Chaucer's phrase, *The Parson's Tale*, l. 157).

18 My text for the English translation is *The Comedy of Dante Alighieri*, tr. Dorothy L. Sayers, Penguin Classics, I (Baltimore, 1960).

19 *The Cambridge Italian Dictionary*. The Italian text consulted is *La Divina Commedia di Dante Alighieri*, ed. C. H. Grandgent, rev. ed. (Boston, 1933).

20 Thomas G. Bergin's colloquial translation of *malebolge* in his *Dante* (New York, 1965), p. 219. Literally it means "evil (*male-*) sacks (*bolge*)." *Bolgia* also means "pocket" and "wallet" (*The Cambridge Italian Dictionary*). See also Miss Sayers' comments, pp. 185-86.

21 Charles Allen Dinsmore makes an excellent point: "Dante believed that the penalty of sin is to dwell in it. Man is punished by his sins rather than for them. Hell is to live in the evil character one has made for himself. Therefore we have but to observe the appearance, the action, the feelings of the doomed, to know the poet's conception of sin" (*The Teachings of Dante* [Westminster, 1902], p. 94).

22 Sayers, p. 185. A similar image occurs in the description of the wrathful and the sullen (VII). They are placed in the slough of the Styx, the sullen submerged below the wrathful, for "the sullen hatreds lie gurgling, unable even to express themselves for the rage that chokes them" (Sayers, p. 114).

23 Sayers, p. 199.

24 Dante's word is *fondo*, which means "bottom, lowest part, end" (*The Cambridge Italian Dictionary*). I interpret the word here in the literal as well as the anatomical sense.

25 One negligible exception occurs at the end of Canto XXI. The devils stick their tongues out at their leader as a form of salute, to which their leader responds with a fart (lines 136-39).

26 I.xxxvi.117. My text for the English translation is *The Histories of Gar-*

gantua and Pantagruel, tr. J. M. Cohen, Penguin Classics (Baltimore, 1963).

27 Another notable example of scatological humor is Panurge's filthy prank upon a Parisian lady for her refusal to accommodate his desire (II.xxi-xxii).

28 Gargantua's "invention of an arse-wiper" is also an indirect satire of this kind as may be seen in the following digression by the child-giant to his father: "Do not imagine that the felicity of the heroes and demigods in the Elysian Fields arises from their asphodel, their ambrosia, or their nectar, as those ancients say. It comes, in my opinion, from their wiping their arses with the neck of a goose, and that is the opinion of Master Duns Scotus too" (I.xiii.69).

29 Another philosopher ferments "a great tub of human urine in horse-dung" to produce a distillation with which he lengthens the lives of kings and princes "by a good six or nine feet" (V.xxii.651).

30 The attack on the monks includes a lampoon of King Lent drawn in a series of similes (some 174 of them) of which the scatological comparisons are the most damaging and sarcastic, e.g., "His urine like a popefig. . . . His arse-hole like a crystal mirror. . . . If he farted, it was brown cow-hide gaiters" (IV.xxix-xxxii).

CHAPTER 2

1 The proportion of scatological jests in collections of jests and facetiae of popular writings is as follows: *A Hundred Merry Tales* (1526) contains three scatological jests (nos. 7, 26, 39) out of 100 jests (in *A Hundred Merry Tales and Other English Jestbooks of the Fifteenth and Sixteenth Centuries,* ed. P.M. Zall [Lincoln, Nebraska, 1963]—hereafter cited as *English Jestbooks*); *Howleglas* (1528?) 9 (nos. 7, 11, 12, 16, 23, 27, 29, 44, 45) out of 47 (in *English Jestbooks*); *Tales and Quick Answers* (1535?) 7 (nos. 18, 28, 36, 89, 95, 101, 110) out of 113 (in *English Jestbooks*); *Conceits, Clinches, Flashes, and Whimzies* (1639) 7 (nos. 42, 85, 122, 123, 124, 151, 277) out of 287 (in *Shakespeare Jest-Books,* ed. W. Carew Hazlitt [New York: Burt Franklin (1964?)], III); *Oxford Jests* (1671) 5 (nos. 119, 162, 385, 426, 444) out of 583; *Cambridge Jests* (1674) 7 (nos. 27, 75, 177, 202, 205, 293, 324) out of 347; *Coffee-House Jests* (1677) 8 (nos. 10, 51, 261, 295, 330, 332, 333, 376) out of 397. The proportion of scatological pieces (satirical and non-satirical) in collections of literary epigrams is as follows: Everard Guilpin, *Skialetheia* (1598) 3 (nos. 7, 23, 68) out of 70 epigrams; William Goddard, *A Neaste of Waspes* (Dort, 1615) 8 (nos. 10, 45, 76, 77, 88, 89, 92, 94) out of 102. Since I find it too lengthy to identify the pieces by descriptive titles, I have not included statistics for those collections, popular and literary, with no number assigned for each piece.

2 Page 13. Other examples of this kind are no. 124, *Conceits, Clinches, Flashes and Whimzies* (1639), *Shakespeare Jest-Books,* III, 33; no. 52, "A Jest retorted," [Archibald Armstrong], *A Banquet of Jests New and Old* (1657), p. 131; no. 205, *Cambridge Jests,* pp. 79-80; "On Kitching Stuff," *The Complaisant Companion,* p. 15.

3 *English Jestbooks,* pp. 200-01. Some other jests of this kind are no. 23, *Howleglas,* "How Howleglas deceived the Jews with dirt," and no. 9, *Merry*

Tales Made by Master Skelton (1567), "How Skelton handled the friar that would needs lie with him in his inn," both in *English Jestbooks*, pp. 189-92, 335-36.

4 *The Jests of Scogin* (1626), *Shakespeare Jest-Books*, II, 112.

5 Some other examples are no. 36, "Of the merchant that made a wager with his lord," *Tales and Quick Answers*, in *English Jestbooks*, pp. 269-70; "The Foole of Cornewall," *Jacke of Dovers Quest of Inquirie* (1604), and "How *Scogin* and his wife made an Heire," *The Jests of Scogin*, in *Shakespeare Jest-Books*, II, 345-46, 93-94; nos. 122, 123, *Conceits, Clinches, Flashes and Whimzies*, in *Shakespeare Jest-Books*, III, 32-33; no. 35, "A Gentleman Usher that let a fart," *A Banquet of Jests*, p. 20; no. 202, *Cambridge Jests*, pp. 76-77; nos. 332, 376, *Coffee-House Jests*, pp. 196, 221.

6 *Shakespeare Jest-Books*, III, 67-68. Some other examples are no. 7 ("How Howleglas creeped into a bee hive . . ."), no. 12 ("How Howleglas made a sick child shite . . ."), no. 16 ("How Howleglas won the king's fool of Casimir . . ."), no. 44 ("How Howleglas . . . was sick . . ."), *Howleglas*, in *English Jestbooks*, pp. 162-64, 170-71, 176-77, 232-34; no. 95, "Of the widow's daughter that was sent to the abbot with a couple of capons," *Tales and Quick Answers*, in *English Jestbooks*, p. 311; "How *Scogin* gave one a medicine to make him go to it," *The Jests of Scogin*, in *Shakespeare Jest-Books*, II, 87; "How drunken Mullins of Stratford dreamed he found gold," *Pasquils Jests* (1604), in *Shakespeare Jest-Books*, III, 43; "A Scotch man and his Mistris," *A Banquet of Jests*, pp. 167-68; no. 177, *Cambridge Jests*, p. 67.

7 *The First Hundred of Epigrammes* (1556), *John Heywood's Works and Miscellaneous Short Poems*, ed. Burton A. Milligan, Illinois Studies in Language and Literature, XLI (Urbana, 1956), p. 132. Cf. Thomas More, "On Breaking Wind from the Greek," *The Latin Epigrams of Thomas More* (1518), ed. Leicester Bradner and Charles A. Lynch (Chicago, 1953), p. 150; "On a Fart," John Cotgrave, *Wits Interpreter* (1655), p. 273; "Aenigma XXXVIII [A Fart]," *Thesaurus Aenigmaticus* (1725-26), p. 35. See also the humorous "An Encomium [of a Fart]," *Wits Recreation* (1640), reprinted in *Facetiae* (London, 1817), II, 395-96. The popularity of this ironic encomium may be seen in its repeated appearance under different titles with slight changes in the poem: "On a Fart," *Westminster Drolleries* (1671-72), ed. J. W. Ebsworth (Boston, Lincolnshire, 1875), pp. 127-29; "On a Fart," *Wit and Drollery* (1682), pp. 145-46; "The best Perfume, or a Paradox in Praise of Farting," *Athenian Sport* (1707), pp. 114-15.

8 *Epigrammes and Elegies* (Middleborough [1593-94?]), sig. B2. Some other examples are Guilpin, no. 23, "Of Sextilius," *Skialetheia*, sig. A7; Goddard, nos. 88, 94, *A Neaste of Waspes*, sigs. G2^{v}, G4; and nos. 20, 34, *A Mastif Whelp* (1599), sigs. I2^{v}, K4-K4^{v}; Henry Parrot, no. 72, *Laquei Ridiculosi* (1613), sig. D2^{v}; Thomas Freeman, "In Salonum," *Rubbe, and a Great Cast* (1614), sig. G4^{v}; Herrick, no. 551 ("Way in a crowd"), no. 572 ("Upon Umber"), no. 795 ("Upon Bice"), no. 987 ("The Quintell"), *Hesperides* (1648), *The Complete Poetry of Robert Rerrick*, ed. J. M. Patrick (New York, 1963), pp. 266, 273, 349, 404 (hereafter cited as *Hesperides*); "Upon a Fart

Unluckly Let," *Musarum Deliciae; or, The Muses Recreation* (1656), reprinted in *Facetiae*, I, 40-42.

9 No. 89, *A Neaste of Waspes*, sigs. G2v-G3.

10 No. 428, *Hesperides*, p. 218 and n.; two other examples are nos. 237 and 650. Other scatological pieces in *Hesperides* include nos. 5, 131, 636, 890. Some other examples of scatological humor are Parrot, "Subita, magis quarenda," *The Mastive, or Younge-Whelpe of the Olde Dogge* (1615), sig. F3, and "Somnus decipiens," *Cvres for the Itch* (1626), sig. D2; Thomas Wroth, no. 91, *The Abortive of an Idle Houre: or a Centurie of Epigrams* (1620), sig. K; Richard Flecknoe, "The Hollanders neatnesse," *The Diarium, or Journall* (1656), pp. 9-10; "Upon a House of Office over a River, set on fire by a coale of Tobacco," *Choyce Drollery* (1656), ed. J. W. Ebsworth (Boston, Lincolnshire, 1876), pp. 33-37; "Mr. Smith's Taking a Purge," *Wit Restor'd* (1658), reprinted in *Facetiae*, I, 150-52; *On the Praise of Fat Men*, in *Wit and Drollery*, pp. 231-47; "The Country Squire and his Man John," *The Muse in Good Humour*, 5th ed. (Dublin, 1745), pp. 1-4. Wittier examples include riddles, "Why lookes he angry?", *Qvips vpon Qvestions* (1600), sigs. C2-C2v; "Aenigma CXII [A Glyster]," *Thesaurus Aenigmaticus*, pp. 110-11.

11 An outstanding example is Skelton's *The Tunning of Elinour Rumming* (c.1508). Scatology also helps establish a coarsely humorous tone as in burlesque verse, e.g., in the burlesque blazon of Flecknoe's "On Madam Tumbril," *A Collection of the Choicest Epigrams and Characters* (1673), p. 75. Cf. "On his Beautiful Mistriss," "On Fat Peg," William Hickes, *London Drollery* (1673), pp. 43-45, 62.

12 *The Complete Poems of John Skelton*, ed. Philip Henderson, 3rd ed. (London, 1959), pp. 150-64. In the absence of line numbers in the text, I am using page numbers instead.

13 Rochester's "My Lord All-Pride" is another personal satire in the same tradition. Like Skelton, Rochester stresses the animal nature of his enemy, his ill smell, his ugly appearance, his poor wit, and so on. Scatology appears in a cluster and is particularly powerful because of the relatively short length of the poem (30 lines):

> . . . his starved fancy, is compell'd to take,
> Among the *Excrements* of others wit,
> To make a stinking *Meal* of what they shit.
> So *Swine*, for nasty *Meat*, to *Dunghil* run,
> And toss their gruntling *Snowts* up when they've done.
> (ll. 8-12)

(*Rochester's Poems on Several Occasions* [1680], ed. James Thorpe [Princeton, 1950], p. 144.) Cf. Marston's scatological jibe at his literary enemy Hall in *Satire* III. 111-14 and *Satire* X. 59-66 in *The Scourge of Villanie* (1598), *The Poems of John Marston*, ed. Arnold Davenport (Liverpool, 1961), pp. 114, 165.

14 *Under-wood* (1640), *The Complete Poetry of Ben Jonson*, ed. William B. Hunter, Jr. (New York, 1963), p. 158. Some other examples are Goddard, nos. 45, 76, 77, *A Neaste of Waspes*, sigs, E, F4-F4v; Henry Hutton, no. 47, "To

his inconstant mistrisse," *Follie's Anatomie* (1619), *Early English Poetry, Ballads, and Popular Literature of the Middle Ages,* Percy Society (New York: Johnson Reprint Corp., 1965), VI, 43; Davies, no. 43, "In Publium," *Epigrammes,* sig. D2; John Harington, "Against *Lynus,* a Wryter, that found fault with the *Metamorphosis," The Letters and Epigrams of Sir John Harington,* ed. N. E. McClure (Philadelphia, 1930), p. 166–hereafter to be cited as *Letters and Epigrams.*

15 We may note that even when a poem treats an individual as in Jonson's epigram, it often takes on the character of general satire. Unlike an epitaph or eulogy, where the author identifies a specific person, in satirical epigrams (and more frequently in scatological ones) the author often adopts the practice of assigning a Latin name (as in Davies' epigram, no. 43) to make the satire appear less personal and more general. (Of course, in some poems, Latin name or no, we cannot mistake the personal nature of the satire because of specific allusions in the poem, as in Harington's epigram no. 47.) Thus when discussing personal satire, we should keep in mind the possible implication of general satire. We know that many authors occasionally write general satire under the pretense of satirizing an individual (as in character-writing). Davies reminds us that his epigram "taxeth vnder a particular name,/ A generall vice that merites publike blame" (no. 1, "Ad Musam," *Epigrammes,* sig. A3). Cf. Parrot, "Casus mutatus," *Cures for the Itch,* sig. E5.

16 *The Works of Thomas Nashe,* ed. Ronald B. McKerrow (London, 1910), III. For a full account of the quarrel, see McKerrow, V, 65-110.

17 Page 62. Cf. Harvey's railing against Nashe in *Pierces Supererogation* (1593): "Phy vpon arrant knauery, that hath neuer sucked his fill of most-odious Malice: or, Out-vpon scurrilous, & obscene Villany, nusled in the boosome of filthiest filth, and hugged in the armes of the abominablest hagges of Hell," *The Works of Gabriel Harvey,* ed. Alexander B. Grosart, Huth Library (New York: AMS Press, 1966), II, 267.

18 "Slavonian, *term of contempt,*" McKerrow's note, V, 342.

19 "Gub" ("gub-shite"): not in *NED.*

20 Harvey, too, scorns Nashe's works as excrements. Cf. ". . . your pen be so ranke, that it cannot stande vpon any ground, but the soile of Calumny, in the muck-yard of Impudency . . . your tongue soe laxatiue, that it must vtterly vtter a great horrible deale more then all . . ."; "He can raile . . . but the sauour of his railing, is grosely fell, and smelleth noysomly of the pumpe, or a nastier thing" (*Pierces Supererogation,* II, 89, 115). Later in *The Trimming of Thomas Nashe* (1597), Harvey refers to Nashe's newest satire as "thy latest bred excrements," III. 50.

21 Harvey refers to Nashe as an ass (as a pun on "Nashe" and "Ass" [Grosart's note, III, 107]) and pictures Nashe's mouth as the source of his verbal excrement. Cf. ". . . when thou hast wiped thy mouth with thine owne Asse-dung; and thine owne Tounge hath sayd vnto thy Pen, Pen thou art an Asse . . ." (*Pierces Supererogation,* II, 250). On the next page, Harvey, in an ironic encomium on ass, praises "Asses dung" to be "a sweet nosegay to staunch bloud, a souerain fumigation to expell a dead birth out of the moothers woombe, and a

faire emplaster for a fowle mouth, as it might be for the mouth of Bawdery in ryme, or of Blasphemie in prose." Harvey's "secret allegorie" on Nashe's halitosis in *The Trimming of Thomas Nashe* is of course not an ordinary halitosis but an attempt to discredit Nashe's writings (III, 21-24). Harvey's conception of Nashe's halitosis stems from his conception of Nashe's language as verbal excrements. We might note too the use of scatology in expressing greatest personal insult in the Bible: "But Rabshakeh said unto them, Hath my master sent me to thy master, and to thee, to speak these words? hath he not sent me to the men which sit on the wall, that they may eat their own dung, and drink their own piss with you?" (II Kings 18:27; Isa. 36:12)

22 A less scatological and later example of personal satire is a quarto, "A Hue-and-Cry after Beauty and Vertue" (1685). Harington's *Metamorphosis of Ajax* (1596) (ed. Elizabeth S. Donno [New York, 1962]) also contains personal satire against individuals. Although the personal satire itself is not scatological, it may be considered such, because it appears in an argument for improving a privy. Though Harington refers to his satiric targets (pp. 180-86), he avoids easy identification of persons. Mrs. Donno comments that "Since Harington does adhere to historical sources, apparently relying on a cluster of skilfully selected details to reveal his topical reference, it is impossible in most cases for us to detect the allusion with any certainty; in many instances it must have been equally difficult for his readers, even for those most caught up in the social and political intrigues of the courtly world" (p. 22). Harington, in discussing the satirical elements in his work, assures the reader that "A Jax when he is at his worst, yeelds not a more offensive savour to the finest nostrils, then some of the faults I have noted do, to God and the world" (p. 183). He concludes his work with the couplet, "To keepe your houses sweete, cleanse privie vaults,/ To keepe your soules as sweete, mend privie faults" (p. 186).

23 *The Holy State and the Profane State,* ed. Maximilian G. Walten (New York, 1938), II, 357.

24 *Characters: or, Wit and the World* (1663), sig. C3. Cf. John Tutchin's opening lines in "A Satyr against Whoring," *Poems on Several Occasions* (1685), p. 10:

> Slaves to Debauchery and Lustful Rage,
> That drain the Streets, and prostitute the Stage,
> Begot in heat of Lust on *Hackney* Whores,
> Souls wrapt in Excrements of common Shoars.

25 *Two Essays of Love and Marriage* (1657), p. 54.

26 "A Prostitute or Common Whore," *Characters,* sig. E5^{v}. Cf. a similar figure by Chaucer in *The Parson's Tale* (l.885): "harlotes [low fellows] that haunten bordels of thise fool wommen, that mowe be likned to a commoune gong [privy], where as men purgen hire ordure."

27 *Works of John Taylor the Water Poet* (not included in the Folio Volume of 1630), Spenser Society, III (Manchester, 1876), 32-33. Cf. two prurient poems with scatological lines against the prostitute: "Against the Charmes our *Ballocks* have" (authorship not certain; see Thorpe's note, p. 181) and "As crafty *Harlots,*

use to shrink" (by Etherege?), *Rochester's Poems on Several Occasions,* pp. 73-74, 80.

28 Ordinarily the word "projector" meant a promoter of business ventures and schemes. Though not all projectors were dishonest, most of them apparently were, hence the usual connotation of swindler associated with the word. H. M. Robertson in *Aspects of the Rise of Economic Individualism* (New York, 1959) points out that "so great a nuisance did the fraudulent projector become, that King James, who was himself very receptive to projects and 'plotts,' used the word 'projector' as a general term of abuse along with 'viper' and 'pest' in a speech to Parliament in 1609" (p. 192). (For further discussion on this topic, see Robertson, pp. 189-93.) In *An Essay upon Projects* (1697) Defoe condemns dishonest projectors who "cry it up for a New Invention, gets a Patent for it, divides it into shares" and after pocketing the fund for his "invention" runs away from the investors (pp. 32-35). The word "projector," however, was not always used with the same meaning, so that a particular meaning of the word in a given work must be derived from the context in which it appears.

29 Quoted by Elizabeth S. Donno, *Harington's Metamorphosis of Ajax,* p. 167, n. 35. See Harington's satire on Platt and monopolies in the *Metamorphosis,* pp. 165-68.

30 Benjamin Boyce, *The Polemic Character 1640-1661* (Lincoln, Neb., 1955), p. 83.

31 Ibid.

32 He also sarcastically comments that the projector will "fatten all foure footed beasts without Hay, or Grasse, or any manner of Graine, make bread of Pumpions, and Cucumbers . . . and victuall the King an Army without meat . . ." (sig. B4).

33 Before finishing with social satire, we may note Alexander Radcliffe's *A Call to the Guard by a Drum* in *The Ramble* (1682), "An Anti-Heroic Poem" with a humorous satire on the Redcoats in particular and on the soldiers' lot in general (reprinted in *Rochester's Poems on Several Occasions,* pp. 131-38).

34 Page 1. On the Chaucer reference see n. 42 below.

35 Reprinted in *The Harleian Miscellany* (London, 1810), VII, 141-44.

36 No. 295, *Coffee-House Jests,* p. 176. A few other jests of political satire may be noted here: "How the French King had *Scogin* into his house of office, & shewed him the King of England's picture," *Jests of Scogin,* in *Shakespeare Jest-Books,* II, 144; no. 51, *Coffee-House Jests,* p. 32; no. 14, "A horse pissing into the River," *A Banquet of Jests,* p. 8.

37 Page 61. This poem appears under the title "On a Fart In the Parliament House: By Sir John Suckling" in Thomas D'Urfey's collection of songs, *Pills to Purge Melancholy,* III (1719), 332-33. An expanded version of this poem appears under the title "The Fart Censured in the Parliament House" in *Musarum Deliciae: or, The Muses Recreation* (1656), reprinted in *Facetiae,* I, 66-72. For more examples of similar scatologicial satire on the Parliamentarian party, see the following pieces in *The Rump, or A Collection of Songs and Ballads Made upon Those Who Would Be a PARLIAMENT, and Were but the Rump of an House of Commons, Five Times Dissolv'd* (1660): "The Re-Resurrection of the

Rump: or, Rebellion and Tyranny revived," sigs. Aa-Aa2v; "Fortunate Rising, or the Rump upward," sigs. B5v-B6; "Arsy Versy or, the Second Martyrdom of the RUMP" (signatures disarranged); "Bum-Fodder or Waste-Paper Proper to wipe the *Nations* Rump with, or your Own," sigs. D-D2v; "A Vindication of the Rump: or, the Rump Re-Advanc'd," sigs. D3-D4v; "The Rump Carbon-ado'd," sigs. Ev-E5.

38 "The Preface" to *Animadversions upon the Remonstrants Defence against Smectymnuus* (1641), *Complete Prose Works of John Milton*, I (New Haven, 1953), 662. We may recall that later in *An Apology against a Pamphlet call'd A Modest Confutation of the Animadversions upon the Remonstrant against Smectymnuus* (1642), Milton again defends the use of violent language against Bishop Hall on the same ground, citing as a precedent Christ himself, who, he points out, "speaking of unsavory traditions, scruples not to name the Dunghill and the Jakes . . ." (p. 895) ("Alluding probably to Luke 14:35; Mark 7:15, 19-20, 21-23; and Matt. 15:17," p. 895, n. 146, Frederick L. Taft). In practice, however, even in these two pamphlets, Milton's invective against Hall does not contain enough scatalogy to make it worth our consideration.

39 "Of *Cloacina* and *Sterquitius*," *Letters and Epigrams*, p. 167. See also "A dish of dainties for the Diuell," Harington's satire on the devil written in similar scatological wit, p. 166.

40 Cf. Phineas Fletcher's description of the Roman church in *The Locusts, or Apollyonists* (1627) (II.29):

> When late our whore of Rome was disary'd,
> Strip't of her pall, and skarlet ornaments,
> And all her hidden filth lay broad displayd,
> Her putride pendant bagges, her mouth that sents
> As this of hell, her hands with scabbes array'd,
> Her pust'led skin with ulcer'd excrements;
> Her friends fall off; and those that lov'd her best,
> Grow sicke to think of such a stinking beast:
> And her, and every limbe that touch't her, much detest.

(*The Poetical Works of Giles Fletcher and Phineas Fletcher*, ed. Frederick S. Boas, I [Cambridge, 1908], 148)

41 *Letters and Epigrams*, p. 183.

42 See Norman O. Brown on Luther's conception and treatment of the excremental character of the devil in the chapter "The Protestant Era," *Life Against Death* (New York, 1959), pp. 207-10, 225-26, 229. The association of friars and the devil seems to be of medieval origin. We may recall the nauseating account of Chaucer's summoner in *The Summoner's Prologue* about the future abode of friars, how a friar dreamt that he went to hell and saw a multitude of friars harbored in Satan's "ers." The notion of the devil as the source of all sorts of troubles also seems to be of medieval origin. The devil is seen as the main source of man's woes, a Pandora's box, so to speak. We remember Dante's description of the Cocytus as the "fundament of the world" (*Inf.* XXXII.7), suggesting it as the source of sin and evil. Phineas Fletcher in *The Purple Island*

(1633) refers to sin as "the devils dung" (XII.31). On the title page of John Taylor's *A Reply as True as Steele, to a Rusty, Rayling, Ridiculous, Lying Libell* (1641), there is a picture of the devil in the act of voiding a bearded libeler, with the following couplet as its caption:

The Divell is hard bound and did hardly straine,
To shit a Libeller a knave in graine.

(*Works of John Taylor the Water Poet,* Spenser Society, IV [1877]) This same picture with a few minor changes in detail appears on the title page of *The Devil Turn'd Round-Head* (n. d.) (reproduced in William Holden's *Anti-Puritan Satire 1572-1642* [New Haven, 1954], p. 122).

43 Of the earlier examples, we may cite the fourteenth-century poem, "The Land of Cokaygne."

44 E.g., Goddard, no. 10, "A godlie Father of the romishe sect," *A Neaste of Waspes,* sig. B3v, and no. 385, *Oxford Jests,* p. 106.

45 For example, no. 45, "How Howleglas received his ghostly father," *Howleglas,* in *English Jestbooks,* pp. 234-35, and no. 298, "A Priest and Pears," Roger L'Estrange, *Fables of Aesop and other Eminent Mythologists: with Morals and Reflections* (1724), p. 312.

46 Printed in *The Works of Mr. John Oldham, Together with his Remains* (1722), II, 325-34; also reprinted in [L. Meriton], *Pecuniae Obediunt Omnia,* 2nd ed. (1698), pp. 125-32, and Huntington Brown, *Rabelais in English Literature* (Paris, 1933), pp. 223-28.

47 *The Complete Works of George Gascoigne,* ed. John W. Cunliffe, II (Cambridge, 1910), 245-46.

48 See also "Of Drunkenness," *The English Treasury of Wit and Language,* p. 85; no. 96, *The Abortive of an Idle Houre,* sig. Kv; "The Drunken Humors," *Wits Recreations,* reprinted in *Facetiae,* II, 397-400.

49 Juvenal employs this term in his assault on the decadent matrons of Rome. He believes that these sexual monsters ("haec monstra") were bred partly from moral decadence, which in turn was engendered by "luxury, more savage than war." He brands this luxury as "filthy lucre." As a noun "obscena" means "the excrements" (*Harper's Latin Dictionary*). Cf. Martial, I.37: "Your bowels' load —and you are not ashamed—you receive in a golden vessel—unhappy urn!/ Bassus, you drink out of crystal; therefore your evacuations are the more costly" (tr. Ker, Loeb Classical Library).

The phrase "filthy lucre" is employed also in the Bible, where it means "tainted" money, referring to "money used for wrong purposes, or to obtain evil ends" (I Tim. 3:3, 8; Titus 1:7, 11; I Pet. 5:2) (Walter L. Wilson, *Wilson's Dictionary of Bible Types* [Grand Rapids, Mich., 1965], p. 181). An earlier example appears in the ninth character of Theophrastus ("Unconscionableness . . . is a neglect of reputation for the sake of filthy lucre . . .") (*The Characters of Theophrastus,* tr. J. M. Edmonds, Loeb Classical Library [Cambridge, Mass., 1953], p. 63). The original word is *aischros,* which means "turpis" and (in a moral sense) "shameful," "base" (Liddell and Scott's *Greek-English Lexicon*).

50 Cf. Dante's phrase "usury as a crime against God's bounty" ("usura offende/ la divina bontade") (*Inf.* XI.95-96).

51 No. 112, *The Scourge of Folly* (1611), *The Complete Works of John Davies of Hereford,* ed. A. B. Grosart, II (Edinburgh, 1878), 21. Bastard also condemns the avaricious by an excremental epithet "filthy muckers" (*Chrestoleros,* VII. 25, 171). Cf.

> Under the Asse tayle thoughe it be no thynge pure
> Yet many seke and grope for the vyle fatnes
> Gatherynge togyther the fowle dunge and ordure
> Such ar they that for treasour and ryches
> Whyle they ar yonge in theyr chefe lustynes
> An agyd woman taketh to theyr wyfe
> Lesynge theyr youth, and shortynge theyr lyfe.

("Of yonge folys that take olde wymen to theyr wyues, for theyr ryches," Alexander Barclay, *The Ship of Fools* [1509], ed. T. H. Jamieson [Edinburgh, 1874], I, 248)

52 "To an Avaricous Person," *A Collection of the Choicest Epigrams* (1673), p. 79. See also his "Of a Rich Miser," *Seventy-Eight Characters* (1677), p. 60. Some other examples are "The Character of a Niggard," *A Strange Horse-Race* (1613), *The Non-Dramatic Works of Thomas Dekker,* ed. A. B. Grosart, Huth Library, III (London, 1885), 335, and "On the Jakes Farmer," [L. Meriton], *Pecuniae Obediunt Omnia,* 2nd ed. (1698), p. 94.

53 No. 184, tr. Robert Hayman, "Certain Epigrams out of the first fovre bookes of . . . John Owen," *Quodlibets,* pp. 34-35.

54 Arthur O. Lovejoy points out that one of the reasons for rejecting Copernican astronomy in the sixteenth and mid-seventeenth centuries was that it elevated the drossy earth (*The Great Chain of Being* [Cambridge, Mass., 1936], pp. 101-02).

The scatological expression of "contemptus mundi" is particularly notable in religious writings. Bernard of Cluny (fl. 1150) in *De Contemptu Mundi* denounces the sinful people and world in images of ill odor, decay, and filth (most of these passages in the poem are quasi-scatological). Among more pointedly scatological expressions we may recall the following examples from other works:

"I count all things *but* loss for the excellency of the knowledge of Christ Jesus my Lord: for whom I have suffered the loss of all things, and do count them *but* dung, that I may win Christ" (St. Paul's assertion, Phil. 3:8).

Joshua Sylvester's *Bartas: His Deuine Weekes and Workes* (1605) contains two notable images—"This Age is sinke of euery former Age,/ Receauing each Sinnes vgliest excrement" (p. 576); and the following passage:

> . . . if thy mind be alwaies fixed all
> On the foule dunghill of this darksome Vale,
> It will partake in the contagious smells
> Of th' vncleane house wherein it droopes and dwells.
> (p. 248)

Another example is Justice's accusation of man's sin in Giles Fletcher's *Christs Victorie in Heaven* (1610):

> Dread Lord of Spirits, well thou did'st devise
> To fling the worlds rude dunghill, and the drosse
> Of the ould Chaos, farthest from the skies,
> And thine owne seate, that heare the child of losse,
> Of all the lower heav'n the curse, and crosse,
> That wretch, beast, caytive, monster Man, might spend,
> (Proude of the mire, in which his soule is pend)
> Clodded in lumps of clay, his wearie life to end.

(*Poetical Works of Giles . . . and Phineas Fletcher,* I, 22)

An example may be found even in popular writings ("Of the World," *The English Treasury of Wit and Language,* p. 308):

> What's this world like to? faith just like
> An Inn-Keepers Chamber-pot, receives all waters,
> Both good and bad, it had been need of such scowring.

55 Edward Sexby concludes his incitement to tyrannicide, *Killing No Murder* (1657), with the following verses from Job 20:6-7: "Though his Excellency mount up to the heavens, and his head reacheth unto the clouds, yet he shall forever perish like his own dung. They that have seen him shall say, 'Where is he?' " (Reprinted in Roberta F. Brinkley's *English Prose of the XVII Century* [New York, 1951], pp. 607-43.)

56 See Thomas Jordan, *A Cure for the Tongue-Evil* (1662) on swearing.

57 No. 59, *A Banquet of Jests,* p. 136. See also no. 134, "Apples and Horse-Turds," L'Estrange, *Fables of Aesop,* pp. 150-51; Gay, no. 35, "The Barley-Mow and the Dunghill," *The Fables* (1728), *The Poetical Works of John Gay,* ed. G. C. Faber (London, 1926), p. 262.

58 "In Lalum," *Chrestoleros* (1598), V.29, 122. Cf. Guilpin, no. 14, *Skialetheia,* sigs. A5-A5v.

59 No. 19, *The Abortive of an Idle Houre* (1620), sig. H. Cf. Davies, no. 12, *Epigrammes,* sig. Bv and Martial, II.42, VI.81. See the comparison of "the base, and the fore-barren braine" to the image of the frozen dunghill melting in the sun, Book I, *Satire* III.1-10, *Virgidemiarum* (1598), *The Collected Poems of Joseph Hall,* ed. A. Davenport (Liverpool, 1949), p. 14.

60 No. 7, *Skialetheia,* sig. A4. For an example of association of *skata* with inferior verse, see "An Epistolary Essay from M. G. to O. B. upon their Mutual Poems," lines 30-43, *Rochester's Poems on Several Occasions,* p. 4.

61 *NED* lists "writs" as "writings," but here it seems to include the possibility of spoken statements, utterances. "Beslaver" means smearing with saliva.

62 *NED.* Cf. "Of flattery," John Cotgrave, *The English Treasury of Wit and Language* (1655), p. 106; Bastard, *Chrestoleros,* VI.20, 142-43. See the image of indigestion, excretion, and privy in Bastard's poem on libel:

> Libel all rawe with indigested spite,
> Whose witt doth droppe inuenymde iniurie.

Whose pen leakes blots of spitefull infamie,
Which the synke of thy paper doth receite.
Why dost thou boast? for if thou had'st don well.
In naughty things twere easie to excell.
(*Chrestoleros*, III.31, 70-71)

Cf. John Andrewes, "Of the Detractor," *The Anatomie of Basenesse* (1615), sigs. E-Ev.

63 I, 239-40. "*Terms (tearmes):* the chief publishing-seasons" (McKerrow's note, V, 352). "*Plodder at Nouerint:* i.e., scrivener or petty lawyer, from the words 'Noverint universi' with which a writ began; *Circumquaque:* i.e., circumlocutions, rigamoroles . . . ; *siluer games:* I know nothing of these games" (McKerrow's notes, IV, 148). Cf. Robert Burton, "Democritus Ivnior to the Reader," *The Anatomy of Melancholy*, 2nd ed. (Oxford, 1624): "A fault that every writer findes, as I doe now and yet faulty themselues, *trium literarum homines*, all theeues pilfer out of old writers to stuffe vp their new comments, scrape *Ennius* dunghills, & out of *Democritus* pitt. . . . By which meanes it comes to passe, *that not only Libraries and shops are full of our putrid papers, but every close stoole and iakes* . . ." (p. 6); also cf. Pope, *Epilogue to the Satires* (1738), *Dialogue* II. 171-80, *Imitations of Horace*, ed. John Butt, *The Poems of Alexander Pope*, Twickenham Ed., IV (London, 1942), 323 (cf. Donne, *Satyr* II. 25-30).

64 Some other examples are Charles Sedley's satire on Richard Blackmore, "Upon the Author of the *Satyr Against Wit*," *The Poetical and Dramatic Works of Sir Charles Sedley*, ed. Vivian De Sola Pinto (London, 1928), I, 46-47; Henry Carey's satire on Ambrose Phillips, "Namby-Pamby," *The Poems of Henry Carey*, ed. Frederick T. Wood (London [1930]), pp. 112-14; Pope, no. 1, "On *F.M.S.* Gent.," *Epigrams from The Grub-Street Journal*, and no. 2, "Epigrams Occasioned by *Cibber's* Verses in Praise of *Nash*," *Minor Poems*, ed. Norman Ault and John Butt, Twickenham Ed., VI, 325, 360. See also Freeman, "In Salium," *Rubbe and a Great Cast* (1614), sig. D, and [John Webster?], "A Rimer," *The Overburian Characters* (1615), ed. W. J. Paylor (Oxford, 1936), p. 80. One of the most violent satires in this group is Oldham's attack "Upon the Author of a Play call'd *Sodom*," a grossly prurient play popularly ascribed to Rochester. Oldham's language is as unrestrained in scatology and prurience as that of *Sodom* in pornography. The poem ends with the following lines:

For such foul, nasty, *Excrements* of *Wit*,
May they ["thy brave works"] condemn'd to th'
publick *Jakes*, be lent,
[(] For me I'd fear the *Piles*, in vengeance sent
Shou'd I with them prophane my *Fundament*)
There bugger wiping *Porters*, when they shite,
And so thy *Book* it self, turn *Sodomite*.

(*Rochester's Poems on Several Occasions*, pp. 129-31)

65 Dr. Johnson, for instance, made this comment: "The beauties of this poem

are well known; its chief fault is the grossness of its images. Pope and Swift had an unnatural delight in ideas physically impure, such as every other tongue utters with unwillingness and of which every ear shrinks from the mention" (*The Lives of the Most Eminent English Poets* [London, 1816], III, 188). More recently Gilbert Highet denounced Book II as an "overarching fountain of filth" ("Dunciad," *Modern Language Review,* XXXVI [1941], 334).

66 All the line references are to the B text of *The Dunciad,* ed. James Sutherland, *The Poems of Alexander Pope,* Twickenham Ed., 2nd ed., V (London, 1953).

67 Page 133, note to lines 264-66.

68 Robert K. Root, *The Dunciad* (Princeton, 1929), p. 33.

69 Aubrey L. Williams, *Pope's Dunciad* (London, 1955), p. 41.

70 Root, p. 15. Cf. "Alexander P—e's *Nosegay:* or, The *Dunciad* Epitomiz'd" in Jonathan Smedley's *Gulliveriana* (to which is added, *Alexanderiana*) (1728), pp. 315-16. Since this poem is not long, I quote it in full.

First *Jove* strains hard to give *Ambrosia* Vent,
And wipes the *Ichor* from his F—da—nt.
C—l's *Vomit,* and his *Mistress's* Discharge
By *Stool* and *Urine,* next are sung at large.
Then with her T—d our *Bard* embrowns *C—l's* Face,
And fills with *Stench* the *Strand's* extended Space.
Eliza's Breasts, in Language most polite,
Are two *Fore Buttocks,* or *Cows Udders* hight.
Ch—d by *C—l* at *Pissing* overcome,
Crown'd with a *Jordan,* stalks contented home.
But who can bear the *Stink* from *muddy* Streams
Of *Fleet-Ditch, rolling Carrion* to the *Thames*?
Or the *foul* Images he draws from *Jakes*?
Or what a Dutchman *plumps* into the Lakes?
Thus *P—e* is dwindled to a Bog-house Wit,
And writes as filthy Stuff, as others sh—.
Who reads *P—e's* Verses, or *Dean Gully's Prose,*
Must a strong *Stomach* have, or else no *Nose.*

71 See Pope's footnote to the Curl's slip into the faeces (II. 70 ff.). He says in part: "the natural connection there is between Libellers and common Nusances. Nevertheless I have often heard our author own, that this part of his Poem was (as it frequently happens) what cost him most trouble, and pleas'd him least: but that he hoped 'twas excusable, since levell'd at such as understand no delicate satire . . ." (pp. 106-07, note to line 70). He also cites in this note Dryden's use of scatology in *Mac Flecknoe* (1682), ll. 47-48, 100-03.

CHAPTER 3

1 *The Poems of Jonathan Swift,* ed. Harold Williams, 2nd ed. (Oxford, 1958), III, 917-18, lines 1-10 (hereafter cited as *Poems*).

2 Page 921, lines 1-10. Cf. the anonymous poem, "The T—D. Humbly presented to the Teeth of Mr. R," *Gentleman's Magazine,* XVIII (1748), 135, lines 16-24:

> To gain materials for thy fabric, man
> Wears out his life in labour; thou'rt the end
> Of all: an emblem thou how vain the toils,
> The pleasures, honours of the world below.
> Full oft we see thee lift thy curling spire,
> Proud, o'er the grave of those who once were prais'd,
> Caress'd and serv'd—a tribute freely paid
> When Flatt'ry's dumb, and from the mould'ring tomb
> Time tears the trophy, and blots out the name.

3 Page 922, lines 23-38. Cf. "The T—D," lines 30-36:

> The greatest, proudest, and the fairest, deign
> Their visits to thy shrine, thy rites perform
> Daily and gladly too. The monarch there
> Low-bending bows the knee, nor kings alone,
> But e'en immortals think thee worth regard,
> For, of the Gods, as antient bards have sung,
> Some were gold-finders, scavengers were some.

4 *The Sin of Wit* (Syracuse, 1950), p. 117.

5 Page 924, lines 89-94. Cf. "The T—D," lines 46-57:

> Nor yet thy pow'r of doing good departs,
> *Phoebus* his influence joining, thee we find,
> In herbs and fruits unnumber'd, spread the field;
> Whence future t—ds shall phoenix-like proceed,
> Born of thy ashes, and a second time
> Our bodies pass; for what is all our food
> But revoluting t—d, fulfilling still
> The circle mark'd by heav'n? The daintiest dame
> May thus the beggar's t—d, in herbs or fruits,
> Disguis'd, to her nice mouth convey, and there
> Chew with high gust, and from refection sweet
> Rise with new life, and bless the rich repast.

6 Tr. Leonard F. Dean (New York, 1952), p. 38.

7 No. 650, *Hesperides,* p. 300.

8 *Epigrams and Satyres* (1608) [reprinted (London?), 1840], pp. 22-23.

9 *The Battle of the Books* contains a couple of scatological references to Bentley, which I mention under intellectual satire.

10 See Williams' notes, *Poems,* III, 783-84, and I, 64-65.

11 Williams, *Poems,* I, 786 n.

12 *The Poetical Works of Abraham Cowley, The Poets of Great Britain* (London, 1807), II, 21.

13 "Dust" here means garbage or refuse, but I think it also carries a euphemistic association with dung in this poem, especially in connection with the "brute" "clad all in brown." A dustman in this context would be not only a garbage man, but also a gold-finder, one who empties privies.

It is interesting to recall that the skin of Yahoos is "of a brown Buff Colour." See also "Dick, *A Maggot*" (1728), *Poems,* III, 785-86. Other pieces on Tighe with a few scatological references include "Mad Mullinix and Timothy," "*Tim* and the *Fables,*" "Tom Mullinex and Dick," and "Dick's *Variety*" (all in *Poems,* III).

14 See *Poems,* I, 67, notes to lines 53, 56, 57.

15 Later, in describing the animal lust of the female Yahoos, Swift employs a similar olfactory image; the female Yahoo, when enamored, emits "a most offensive Smell."

16 *The Prose Works of Jonathan Swift,* ed. Herbert Davis, XII (Oxford, 1955), 218-19 (hereafter cited as *Prose Works*).

17 Ibid., pp. 219-20.

18 Ibid., pp. 220-21.

19 See *A Tale of a Tub,* p. 93 and n.1; and William King's letter to Mrs. Martha Whiteway (9 Nov. 1736): "I cannot indeed much commend *Edinburgh;* and yet the s—ks, which are so much complained of there, are not more offensive than I have found them in every street in this elegant city [Paris], which the *French* say is the mistress of the world . . . ," *The Correspondence of Jonathan Swift,* ed. Harold Williams, IV (Oxford, 1965), 542.

20 Davis, *Prose Works,* XII, xxxiv-xxxv.

21 *Prose Works,* IX, 284.

22 Ibid., p. 378. Cf. Swift's attitude toward the bankers, as shown in *A Short View of the State of Ireland* (1727): "I have sometimes thought, that this Paradox of the Kingdom growing rich, is chiefly owing to those worthy Gentlemen the BANKERS; who, except some Custom-house Officers, Birds of Passage, oppressive thrifty 'Squires, and a few others who shall be nameless, are the only thriving People among us: And I have often wished, that a Law were enacted to hang up half a Dozen *Bankers* every Year; and thereby interpose at least some short Delay, to one further Ruin of *Ireland*" (*Prose Works,* XII, 11). John C. Collins in his biography *Jonathan Swift* (London, 1902) explains why Swift held an antagonistic view toward the bank: "The mania for commercial adventures, which originating in Law's Mississippi Scheme had culminated in the South Sea Bubble, was now invading Dublin. Among other schemes, a project was formed for establishing a National Bank, and was regarded with some favour by some of the leading citizens and many of the petty tradesmen in Dublin. But Swift saw that an institution eminently useful, and indeed necessary, in a prosperous community could only end in ruin and mischief in a community where stock is incommensurate with credit. He determined, therefore, to oppose the scheme; and ridicule was his weapon" (p. 170).

23

> I'm too *profuse* some Cens'rers cry,
> And all I get, I *let it fly:*
> While others give me many a Curse,
> Because too *close* I hold my *Purse.*
> (*Poems,* III, 918, ll. 25-28)

24 Cf.

> This Cave within its Womb confines
> The last Result of all Designs:
> Here lye deposited the Spoils
> Of busy Mortals endless Toils:
> Here, with an easy Search we find
> The *foul Corruptions* of Mankind.
> The wretched Purchase here behold
> Of Traytors who their Country sold.
> This Gulph insatiable imbibes
> The Lawyer's Fees, the Statesman's Bribes.
> Here, in their proper Shape and Mein,
> Fraud, Perjury, and Guilt are seen.
> (*Poems,* III, 921-22, ll. 11-22)

25 See also *An Account of the short Life, sudden Death, and pompous Funeral of Micky Windybank, etc., Prose Works,* IX, 308-10.

26 Williams, *Poems,* III, 828.

27 "The French King suppos'd a Bastard" (*Poems,* I, 10 n.).

28 *"Fistula in Ano"* (*Poems,* I, 10 n.). This historical fact was also mentioned in *A Tale of a Tub,* p. 165 n.2.

29 For the socio-political background of the poem, see Williams, *Poems,* III, 810, 828.

30 "Swift took the name from the answer of the unclean spirit: 'My name is Legion: for we are many.'" Mark 5:9 (*Poems,* III, 829 n.). See also Luke 8:30: "And Jesus asked him, saying, what is thy name? And he said, Legion: because many devils were entered into him."

31 *"Old Glorious.* William III" (*Poems,* III, 835 n.).

32 The editors' note points out that here "Swift parodies the advertisements of quack medicines" (p. 107 n.).

33 Page 156. The "*Northern* Chink or Crany" refers to Scotland (p. 154, n. 5).

34 Minor targets in the satire of the Aeolists include Scottish dissenters and Quakers. The chief of the Aeolists' gods is the *"Almighty-North,"* whose "peculiar Habitation" is the *"Land of Darkness,"* i.e., Scotland, from whence the zealous among English Aeolists bring the "choicest *Inspiration,* fetching it with their own Hands, from the Fountain Head, in certain *Bladders,* and disploding it among the Sectaries in all Nations, who did, and do, and ever will, daily Gasp and Pant after it" (pp. 154-55). As for the Quakers, in a scurrilous image the author makes fun of their allowing women to preach: "It is true . . . that these [rites of delivering oracles in ancient times] were frequently

managed and directed by *Female* Officers, whose Organs were understood to be better disposed for the Admission of those Oracular *Gusts,* as entring and passing up thro' a Receptacle of greater Capacity, and causing also a Pruriency by the Way, such as with due Management, hath been refined from a Carnal, into a Spiritual Extasie. And to strengthen this profound Conjecture, it is farther insisted, that this Custom of *Female* Priests is kept up still in certain refined Colleges of our *Modern Aeolists,* who are agreed to receive their Inspiration, derived thro' the Receptacle aforesaid, like their Ancestors, the *Sibyls*" (p. 157 and n.). In *The Mechanical Operation of the Spirit* (1704) Swift comments on the relationship between sexual excitation and religious enthusiasm more extensively.

35 Page 12. Like Swift in *The Mechanical Operation of the Spirit,* More sees a connection between sex and enthusiasm. Clarence M. Webster, in "Swift and Some Earlier Satirists of Puritan Enthusiasm," comments that More "seems to have thought of the 'new wine, drawn from the cellar' as being symbolic of a very physical urge" (*PMLA,* XLVIII [1933], 1146). More advocates "The Cure of Enthusiasm by *Temperance, Humility,* and *Reason,*" and Webster quotes More's passage ("What is meant by *Temperance*") that deals with "the relations of sex and zeal": "By *Temperance* I understand a measurable Abstinence from all hot or heightning meats or drinks, as also from all venereous pleasures and tactuall delights of the Body, from all softness and effeminacy; a constant and peremptory adhesion to the perfectest degree of *Chastity* in the single life, and of *Continency* in wedlock, that can be attain'd to. For it is plain in sundry examples of *Enthusiasm* above named, that the more hidden and lurking fumes of *Lust* had tainted the Phansies of those Pretenders to *Prophecy* and *Inspiration*" (More, p. 37; Webster, p. 1146). For a fuller discussion of More's work, see Phillip Harth, *Swift and Anglican Rationalism* (Chicago, 1961), pp. 107-15, and Rosenheim, *Swift and the Satirist's Art* (Chicago, 1963), pp. 129-32.

36 "The Lady's Dressing Room," pp. 524-30, "Cassinus and Peter," pp. 593-97, "Strephon and Chloe," pp. 584-93, all in *Poems,* II.

37 *Swift* (New York, 1955), pp. 439-40.

38 "A Modest Defence of 'The Lady's Dressing Room,'" *Restoration and Eighteenth-Century Literature,* ed. Carroll Camden (Chicago, 1963), p. 42. Throughout my discussion of the Celia poems and "Strephon and Chloe," and particularly in regard to the elements of parody in these poems, I am heavily indebted to this excellent article.

39 Ibid., p. 43. The line from *Paradise Lost* (II. 890-91) refers to "Before their eyes in sudden view appear/ The secrets of the hoary Deep—" (*Poems,* II, 528 n.).

40 Davis, p. 43.

41 Ibid., p. 47.

42 Lines 81-88; quoted also by Davis, p. 48. Swift provides a footnote on line 88, identifying it from *Macbeth* (III. iv. 50, 93) (*Poems,* II, 596 n.).

43 Davis, p. 48.

44 Lines 99-106; quoted also by Davis, p. 48.

45 Maurice Johnson declares that "Women in their dressing-room were for Swift a symbol of mankind's vanity, hypocrisy, and imperfection" (p. 114).

46 Davis comments that "We are perhaps expected to recognize in Celia a woman fashioned out of earth and then endowed with beauty and the powers of seduction, with cunning and the arts of flattery . . ." (p. 43).

47 Lines 307-14. In *A Letter to a Young Lady,* Swift makes similar comments: "But, the grand Affair of your Life will be to gain and preserve the Friendship and Esteem of your Husband. . . . You will, in Time, grow a Thing indifferent, and perhaps contemptible, unless you can supply the Loss of Youth and Beauty with more durable Qualities. You have but a very few Years to be young and handsome in the Eyes of the World; and as few Months to be so in the Eyes of a Husband, who is not a Fool; for, I hope, you do not still dream of Charms and Raptures; which Marriage ever did, and ever will put a sudden End to. . . .

"You must, therefore, use all Endeavours to attain some Degree of those Accomplishments, which your Husband most values in other People, and for which he is most valued himself. You must improve your Mind. . . . This must produce in your Husband a true rational Love and Esteem for you, which old Age will not diminish" (*Prose Works,* IX, 89-90).

We may note in the same *Letter* that, contrary to the popular notion of his misogyny, Swift disapproved of the common practice of excluding ladies from conversation when male guests are invited: "As little Respect as I have for the Generality of your Sex, it hath sometimes moved me with Pity, to see the Lady of the House forced to withdraw, immediately after Dinner, and this in Families where there is not much Drinking; as if it were an established Maxim, that Women are incapable of all Conversation" (p. 90). We recall, too, Swift's biting satire on the barbaric mistreatment of the wives in *A Modest Proposal* (1729), in which he declares that his proposal would, among other things, improve men's conduct toward their wives: "Men would become as *fond* of their Wives, during the Time of their Pregnancy, as they are now of their *Mares* in Foal, their *Cows* in Calf, or *Sows* when they are ready to farrow; nor offer to beat or kick them, (as it is too *frequent* a Practice) for fear of a Miscarriage" (*Prose Works,* XII, 115).

48 *Prose Works,* IX, 87. Swift prefaces this remark in language that may strike today's young ladies as outrageously presumptuous and condescending: "You will perhaps be offended when I advise you to abate a little of that violent Passion for fine Cloaths so predominant in your Sex. It is somewhat hard, that ours, for whose Sake you wear them, are not admitted to be of your Council . . ." (p. 87). We should note, however, that there is no hatred toward women and that he is speaking here as a priest counselling a young woman "whose parents and husband were alike Swift's particular friends" (Davis, *Prose Works,* IX, xxvii).

49 "I would have you look upon Finery as a necessary Folly, which all great Ladies did whom I have ever known: I do not desire you to be out of the Fashion, but to be the last and least in it: I expect that your Dress shall be one Degree lower than your Fortune can afford: And, in your own Heart, I would wish

you to be an utter Contemner of all Distinctions which a finer Petticoat can give you; because, it will neither make you richer, handsomer, younger, better natured, more virtuous, or wise, than if it hung upon a Peg" (*Prose Works,* IX, 91).

50 My remark here is based on Kathleen Williams' comments in *Jonathan Swift and the Age of Compromise* (Lawrence, Kansas, 1958): Swift "will have no short-cuts, no false pretence of order or goodness or beauty where none exists; better to face the muddle and imperfection of human life as it really is" (p. 148). I have also benefited from her fine comments on the three poems I have discussed (K. Williams, pp. 150-52).

51 Printed in *Prose Works,* V, 337-40.

52 Swift goes on to remind the reader how Horace instructs us that though "some Actions should not appear as done upon the Stage . . . they may be *recited* with *Pleasure* and *Elegance*" (p. 338). In order to show that "there are ten Times more *slovenly Expressions*" in Horace "than in the whole Poem called the *Lady's Dressing Room*" Swift quotes ten original lines of Horace from his *Ars Poetica* and for the benefit of those who cannot read Latin, he provides a "literal translation," which is scatological (pp. 339-40). Swift here indulges in a kind of dramatic irony. Those who cannot read the original will be forced to rely on the "literal translation" and admit that Horace, "the great *Master of Politeness,*" is at least as bad as Swift, if not worse, missing Swift's satire on them completely, as they had already failed to see the "useful Satyr" in the poem. Those who can read Latin will at once enjoy Swift's joke on his ignorant and indignant critics. (For a fuller discussion, see Davis' article, "A Modest Defence of 'The Lady's Dressing Room,'" pp. 40-42.) For a recent discussion of "The Lady's Dressing Room," "Cassinus and Peter," and "Strephon and Chloe," see Donald Greene, "On Swift's 'Scatological' Poems," *Sewanee Review,* LXXV (1967), 672-89.

53 *Poems,* II, 584-93.

54 *Life Against Death* (New York, 1959), p. 198.

55 The anonymous author declares, ". . . in Women of a more firm strong Constitution, it vents it self intirely in a Talkativeness, hence we have a reason why Women are more Talkative than Men, for as a certain Poet observes, '*Words own Wind to be their Mother,/ Which stop'd at one end, bursts out at t'other.*' Hence comes the usual saying, *tell a tale or let a Fart,* implying the necessity of vent one way or other" (p. 6). See also Goddard, No. 92, "A Revr'end Iudg sitting to rite mens wronges," *A Neaste of Waspes* (1615), sig. G3v.

56 Brown, p. 198; Phyllis Greenacre, "The Mutual Adventures of Jonathan Swift and Lemuel Gulliver," *Psychoanalytic Quarterly,* XXIV (1955), 56.

57 Among earlier examples of this kind of scatological references to polemics, we may recall the violent exchanges between Nashe and Harvey. Swift uses such references in *The Battle of the Books* (1704) in his derisive description of Bentley: "In his right Hand he grasp'd a Flail, and (that he might never be unprovided of an *offensive* Weapon) a Vessel full of *Ordure* in his Left. . . ." In a footnote Swift explains, "The Person here spoken of, is famous for letting

fly at every Body without Distinction, and using mean and foul Scurrilities" (p. 251). Later in Aesop's dream, Bentley appears as "a *Wild Ass* . . . tramping and kicking, and dunging" in his and Phalaris' faces (p. 254). (*The Battle of the Books* is printed in *A Tale of a Tub,* ed. A. G. Guthkelch and D. Nichol Smith, 2nd ed. [Oxford, 1958], pp. 211-58.)

58 Brown, pp. 198-99; Swift, *Prose Works,* IX, 341-42. Scholars have pointed out, however, that *A Letter of Advice to a Young Poet* may not even be by Swift "in toto": see Davis, *Prose Works,* IX, xxiv-xxvii; Louis T. Milic, *A Quantitative Approach to the Style of Jonathan Swift* (The Hague, 1967), pp. 267-69; Cynthia S. Matlack and William F. Matlack, "A Statistical Approach to Problems of Attribution: *A Letter of Advice to a Young Poet,*" *College English,* XXIX (1968), 632.

59 Cf. Swift's sarcastic comments in *A Tale of a Tub* on "the present Relish of Courteous Readers" who patronize inferior authors with the analogy that "a *Fly* driven from a *Honey-pot,* will immediately, with very good Appetite alight, and finish his Meal on an *Excrement*" (p. 207).

60 *Works of Thomas Nashe,* ed. McKerrow, I, 239.

CHAPTER 4

1 My text of *Gulliver's Travels* is edited by Herbert Davis, *Prose Works,* XI. All references are to this edition. Notable scatological passages are found in Book I.i.25, ii.29, v.56; Book II.i.93-94, iii.109, v.119, 124; Book III.v.179-81, vi.188, 190, 191; Book IV.i.223, 224, vi.253-54, vii.262-63, viii.266.

2 Various comments have been made on this episode. Robert Hunting in *Jonathan Swift* (New York, 1967) cites this passage as "one of the several instances in the *Travels* of satire on travel books and travelers" and suggests that "Swift, through Gulliver, is here mainly protesting the ridiculous traveler who reports everything about his trip, even details about his bowel movements" (p. 99). See also C. J. Rawson, "Gulliver and the Gentle Reader," *Imagined Worlds,* ed. Maynard Mack and Ian Gregor (London, 1968), where he discusses this passage as an example of Swift's asserting himself on the audience, his "self-conscious sniping at the reader's poise." He suggeests that "it is difficult not to sense behind Gulliver's self-apology a small egocentric defiance from the real author" (p. 56). John D. Seelye thinks that Swift in Book I satirizes Hobbes' theory of government based on absolutism and suggests that this episode in the temple as well as the earlier one on the cart (I.i.25) are parodic parallels to Hobbes' definition of liberty ("Hobbes' *Leviathan* and the Gigantism Complex in the First Book of *Gulliver's Travels,*" *Journal of English and Germanic Philology,* LX [1961], 236). An interesting possibility is offered in a humorous pamphlet, *A Key, Being Observations and Explanatory Notes, upon the Travels of Lemuel Gulliver* (1726), in which the anonymous author draws our attention to Gulliver's description of his Lilliputian house ("there stood an ancient Temple, esteemed to be the largest in the whole Kingdom, which having been polluted some Years before by an unnatural Murder, was, according to the Zeal of those People, looked upon as Prophane, and therefore had been applied to common Use, and all the Ornaments and Furniture carried away" [I.i.27]) and observes:

"The *ancient Temple* here described, *polluted some Years ago by an unnatural Murder,* bears so near a Resemblance to the *Banquetting-House* at *White-Hall,* before which Structure, King Charles I was Beheaded, that I must freely own I cannot find any other Pile in this Kingdom more *à propos* to Mr. *Gulliver's* Allusion" (pp. 7-8). Without expert knowledge on political satire in *Gulliver's Travels,* I am unable to make any intelligent comment on this and other opinions. It seems to me, however, that the particular description of the temple raises a strong possibility of incidental allusion to the murder of Charles I, but I am not prepared to trace this line of inquiry with any degree of certainty. The description, in reference to the narrative itself, is certainly consonant with the critical mood toward the Lilliputian court.

3 A few critics have pointed out biographical and political significance in this famous fire. C. H. Firth supposes the episode to refer to Swift's failure to obtain preferment in the Church because of Queen Anne's objection to the *Tale of a Tub* ("The Political Significance of *Gulliver's Travels,*" *Proceedings of the British Academy,* IX [1919-1920], 241). Arthur E. Case sees the incident, however, as "Swift's defense of the Tories' illegal negotiation" of the Peace of Utrecht ("Personal and Political Satire in *Gulliver's Travels,*" *Four Essays on "Gulliver's Travels"* [Gloucester, Mass. 1958], pp. 75-76). While taking Case's side, Irvin Ehrenpreis disagrees with him on the supposed allusion to Gulliver's action. Case thinks Gulliver's experience alludes to Oxford's difficulties with the Queen (Case, pp. 75-76); Ehrenpreis thinks it refers to Bolingbroke (*The Personality of Jonathan Swift* [London, 1958], p. 88). This issue is reviewed also by Milton Voigt, *Swift and the Twentieth Century* (Detroit, 1964), pp. 81-82.

4 Rawson refers to this passage as another instance of Swift's "self-conscious sniping at the reader's poise . . . a variant instance of mock-friendly rubbing-in, for the 'gentle Reader's' benefit . . . where the particularity of travel-writers is part of the joke" (p. 56).

5 This revelation of hitherto unnoticed facts or exposure of reality beneath a pleasing surface by careful examination, often through magnification of details, is of course a familiar device of didacticism and satire. In the following passage we see the use of this technique in Robert Burton's "Cure of Loue-Melancholy" for the purpose of correcting a romantic point of view that claims there are no unpleasant facts to be found in beauty. Swift follows the same technique in the Celia poems. The passage is marked by exaggeration of ugly details characteristic of satiric and didactic writings: "To conclude with *Chrysostome,* 'when thou seest a faire and beautifull person, a comely woman, hauing bright eyes, a merrie countenance, a shining lustre in her looke, a pleasant grace, wringing thy soule, and increasing thy concupiscence; bethinke with thy selfe that it is but earth thou louest, a meere excrement, which so vexeth thee, which thou so admirest, and thy raging soule will be at rest. Take her skinne from her face, and thou shalt see all lothsomnesse vnder it, that beauty is but a superficiall skinne and bones, nerues, sinewes: suppose her sicke, now rivel'd, hoarie-headed, hollowed-cheeked, old; within shee is full of filthie fleame, stinking, putride, excrementall stuffe: snot and sneuill in her nostrils, spittle in her

mouth, water in her eyes, what filth in her braines,' etc. Or take her at best, & looke narrowly vpon her in the light, stand neare her, nearer yet, and thou shalt perceiue almost as much, and loue lesse, as *Cardan* well writes, *minus amant, qui acute vident.* . . . If he see her neare, or looke exactly . . . he shall find many faults in Physiognomie, an ill colour, ill forme, one side of the face likely bigger then the other, crooked nose, bad eyes, prominent veines, concavities about the eyes, wrinkles, pimpels, red streekes, frechons [freckles], haires, warts, neues, inequalities, roughnesse, scabredity, palenesse, yellownes, and as many colours as are in a Turkicocks necke, many indecorums in their other parts . . ." (*The Anatomy of Melancholy,* 2nd ed. [Oxford, 1624], p. 442).

6 As members of the Academy of Lagado, a "research" establishment, "projectors" takes on a specialized meaning of experimenters, theoreticians, and advocates of (to Swift) chimerical schemes with little possibility of benefiting the public. Swift's satire here is indirectly applicable to all dishonest projectors and directly to intellectually myopic visionaries (experimental, theoretical, medical, social, political "scientists") engaged in (in Swift's view) useless projects. (See my discussion of earlier examples of attack on projectors, pp. 35-37.)

7 *Correspondence of Jonathan Swift,* ed. Harold Williams, III (Oxford, 1963), 110, quoted by Harold Williams in the "Introduction" to *Gulliver's Travels, Prose Works,* XI, xx.

8 Ibid., III, 179, quoted by Williams, *Prose Works,* XI, xxi.

9 See Marjorie Nicolson and Nora M. Mohler's valuable study, "The Scientific Background of Swift's *Voyage to Laputa,*" in Miss Nicolson's *Science and Imagination* (Ithaca, New York, 1956), p. 139. Harold Williams comments that "A French writer whom Swift knew well was Rabelais. A copy of his works, annotated by Swift, appeared in the sale catalog. It is in the Voyage to Laputa that the influence of Rabelais is chiefly traceable" ("Introduction" to *Gulliver's Travels, Prose Works,* XI, xv).

10 For a comparison of the two versions, see *Science and Imagination,* pp. 148-49.

11 Ibid., p. 142.

12 For a comparison, see *Science and Imagination,* p. 143.

13 See *The Grand Mystery, or Art of Meditating over an House of Office, Restor'd and Unveil'd; After the Manner of the Ingenious Dr. S—ft* (1726), p. 6. This anonymous pamphlet is another example of scatological humor whose character is suggested in the description of the booklet that appears after the title quoted above: "With Observations Historical, Political and Moral; On the Dignity, Usefulness, and Pleasantness of that Study. With several New Improvements, and Proposals for better accommodating the Nobility and Gentry, of both Sexes, in their Natural Necessities, and for making LONDON the most Magnificent City in the World." A short passage may be cited here as an example: "Happy indeed had it been for him [Caesar] . . . if . . . instead of the Bowels of Brutes, he had consulted the Dung of Men. . . . Had he only appointed trusty and intelligent Visiters, to inspect their [senators'] several Places of Ease, he would have been sensibly forewarn'd of the dangerous Mel-

ancholy of *Brutus*'s Temper, of the malignant Humors that run through *Cassius*'s whole Frame; and would have seen the figure of *Casca*'s Dagger in a T—d" (p. 7).

14 Cf.

> The Statesman rakes the Town to find a Plot,
> And dreams of Forfeitures by Treason got.
> Nor less Tom-T—d-Man of true Stateman mold,
> Collects the City Filth in search of Gold.
> ("On Dreams" [1724], *Poems*, II, 364, lines 19-22)

15 An earlier expression of Swift's attitude toward "the science of governing" appears in *An Enquiry into the Behavior of the Queen's Last Ministry* (1715), *Prose Works*, VIII, 138-39. See also Rawson, p. 72.

16 If Swift's Yahoo strikes us as being excessively foul, we may note that its counterpart appears in certain travel books of Swift's time, as pointed out by R. W. Frantz in "Swift's Yahoos and the Voyagers," *Modern Philology*, XXIX (1931), 49-57: "Lionel Wafer, for example, whose *A New Voyage and Description of the Isthmus of America* (1699) was owned by Swift, told of monkeys, some of which 'have Beards, others are beardless,' skipping 'from Bough to Bough. . . . chattering, and, if they had opportunity, pissing down purposely on our Heads'" (Frantz, p. 52). Frantz also quotes a passage from William Dampier's *Voyages and Descriptions* (1699), a copy of which Swift also owned: "The Monkeys that are in these Parts are the ugliest I ever saw. . . . They were a Great Company dancing from Tree to Tree, over my Head. . . . Some broke down dry Sticks and threw at me; others scattered their Urine and Dung about my Ears . . ." (Frantz, p. 52). If Swift modeled the Yahoo on these monkeys, it is to the credit of his imagination that he created in the Yahoo not merely a filthy creature but a powerful image of nonreason and basic animal drives useful to his satiric purposes.

17 I borrow Roland M. Frye's phrase in his excellent article, "Swift's Yahoo and the Christian Symbols for Sin" (p. 205). In this article he emphasizes the religious overtone of the fourth voyage, in particular the religious connotations of scatology as employed in the description of the Yahoos. He shows the common associations of stink, filth, and deformity with sin in the Bible and seventeenth-century sermons (pp. 210-14). He also suggests the possibility of a satire on Shaftesburian theories of man's natural benevolence: "That Swift regarded theories of natural benevolence as preliminary to moral anarchy, is evidenced by his sermon 'On the Testimony of Conscience,' as well as by other strains of his work. The results of these theories would be the overthrow of individual honesty and virtue. With this in mind, it would seem quite possible that Swift conceived the 'Voyage to the Houyhnhnms' as Christian apologetics, among other things, and that he incorporated into it a sharp satiric attack upon a theologically dangerous doctrine—in this case, upon the conception of man as naturally inclined to goodness. That such an attack would be closely allied with Augustan theology need not be emphasized" (*Journal of History of the Ideas*, XV [1954], 205). Though I am treating the fourth voyage mainly as an intellectual-moral satire rather than

a religious satire, I agree that the conventional religious connotations of scatology, e.g., excrement and filth as metaphors for sin, should not be ignored "for a full understanding of Swift's intent" (p. 217). For a full discussion of the various meanings of "reason" and "nature" in Book IV, see Rawson, pp. 69-79.

18 Cf. Swift's humorous etymological association of "the Latin word *Turpis*" (which "signifieth *nasty*, or *filthy*") with turd and piss in *A Discourse to Prove the Antiquity of the English Tongue* (1765), *Prose Works*, IV, 232. Two other scatological words he cites are *Cloaca* (p. 232) and Ajax (p. 233). Davis describes the *Discourse* as "a sort of learned joke, a parody of philological scholarship" (p. xxxviii).

19 Cf. Sheridan's description of "the Gluttony, Laziness and Luxury of a *Hog*," the archetype of swinish men: "From him are descended your pamper'd Citizens, and others, whose chief Exercise consists in Eating and Drinking: They are very easily distinguished by the Plumpness and Rotundity of their *Dewlap*, the *Torosity* of their *Necks* and *Breasts*, and the *Prominence* of their *Abdomen*," no. 14, "Prometheus's Art of Man-making: And the Tale of the T–d," *The Intelligencer* (1729), p. 151.

20 This is Martin Price's useful phrase, *Swift's Rhetorical Art* (New Haven, 1953), p. 105. See also his comments on the close relation between "the condition of the body" and "the moral estate of man," pp. 83-84.

21 "Holding garlic and rue in . . . mouth and smoking tobacco" were thought to be a safeguard against bubonic plague and its attendant smell of decaying flesh; see Defoe's *Journal of the Plague Year* (1722) (London, 1927), p. 112. Since his departure from Houyhnhnmland, Gulliver acts like a man who is afraid of becoming infected with a disease from his fellowmen. We may recall that when the good Portuguese Captain offers his best suit, Gulliver refuses it, "abhorring to cover myself with any thing that had been on the Back of a *Yahoo*." Instead he settles with the Captain's "two clean Shirts, which having been washed since he wore them, I believed would not so much defile me. These I changed every second Day, and washed them myself" (IV.xi.288).

22 Deane Swift, *An Essay upon the Life, Writings, and Character of Dr. Jonathan Swift* (London, 1755), pp. 218-21; cited by Louis A. Landa, "The Critical Significance of Biographical Evidence: Jonathan Swift," *English Institute Essays 1946* (New York, 1947), p. 32 and by Frye (p. 203). See also Landa, p. 35 and Frye, p. 202.

23 John Traugott, "A Voyage to Nowhere with Thomas More and Jonathan Swift: *Utopia* and *The Voyage to the Houyhnhnms*," *Sewanee Review*, LXIX (1961), 562.

24 Price, p. 107.

25 Swift makes similar comments in *Further Thoughts on Religion* (1765): ". . . their [animal] species never degenerates in their native soil, except they happen to be enslaved or destroyed by human fraud: But men degenerate every day [since the Fall], merely by the folly, the perverseness, the avarice, the tyranny, the pride, the treachery, or inhumanity of their own kind" (*Prose Works*, IX, 264). In "The Beasts Confession to the Priest" (1732), Swift accuses Aesop of "libelling" the beasts by making them act like men, because the beasts

are made to appear as bad as men. In a characteristic turnabout, however, he suggests that perhaps the moralist intends a compliment on man, "For . . . he [Aesop] owns, that now and then/ Beasts may *degen'rate* into Men" (*Poems* II, 608, lines 219-20). One of the reasons the Houyhnhnms want Gulliver to leave their land is their fear of his further degenerating the Yahoos (IV.x.279).

26 See Rawson, pp. 51-69, for his cogent argument that in Swift's major satires "a central Swiftian personality is always actively present, and makes itself felt" (p. 55).

27 "Andrew Marvell," *Selected Essays* (New York, 1932), p. 252.

CONCLUSION

1 Harold Williams declares that "During Swift's life, and after, any witty, grotesque, or indecent piece, of Irish origin and uncertain parentage, was ascribed to the great Dean . . . as if by a standing affiliation order," *Poems,* I, xvii. See also Herbert Davis, "Problems in the Canon of Swift," *English Institute Essays 1942* (New York, 1943), pp. 121-22, 134-35. Some of these ascribed pieces include such examples of scatological humor as *The Benefit of Farting* (1722), *The Blunderful Blunder of Blunders* (1722?), *A Dissertation upon Pissing* (1726), and *Human Ordure, Botanically Considered* (1733). Neither Teerink and Scouten nor Herbert Davis lists or prints any of these pieces in the Swift canon. Dobrée, however, seems to consider one of these as Swift's. He says, "In *Human Ordure, Botanically Considered*—if it is his, and a good case can be made out for its being so—he is trying to humorize it . . . ," *English Literature in the Early Eighteenth Century,* p. 462. The following is a sample of the scatological humor in *Human Ordure: "Daniel Bournbeck,* the famous *Dutch* Fencing-master, told all his Scholars (from one of whom I had the Story) that his *Faeces* always came from him in one solid straight line, but when it touched the Ground it broke exactly in the middle, and divided into two; and the extremities of each falling across one another slanting, represented the most regular posture of the crossing of two Foils or Rapiers, at the first onset or meeting" (p. 28).

2 I borrow this definition of laughter from Erich Segal, *Roman Laughter: The Comedy of Plautus* (Cambridge, Mass., 1968), p. vii.

3 Brian Vickers, "Introduction," *The World of Jonathan Swift,* ed. Brian Vickers (Oxford, 1968), p. 16.

4 Geoffrey Hill, "Jonathan Swift: The Poetry of 'Reaction'," *The World of Jonathan Swift,* p. 209. Norman Brown also discusses this poem in *Life Against Death,* pp. 200-01. Brown's comments on Swift's reference to the Roman myth are much more helpful in understanding the scatological elements of the poem.

Index